The Ten Truths of Wealth Creation

How to Achieve Your Money Goals
Sooner and Safer
In Good Times and Bad

The Ten Truths of Wealth Creation

How to Achieve Your Money Goals
Sooner and Safer
In Good Times and Bad

BY JOHN E. GIROUARD

Bethesda, Maryland

To order copies:
John E. Girouard
4800 Montgomery Square, Suite M-25
Bethesda, MD 20814
(240) 482-4000
info@JohnGirouard.com
or visit www.JohnGirouard.com

First Edition
Printed in the United States of America

Contents

Dedicated to my Mom and Dad,
Claire and Gerry Girouard,
who taught me the fundamentals of money;
To my wife, Colleen,
for her constant support in everything I do;
And to my children, Caitlin and Coley,
who have brought so much joy to my life.

About the Author

JOHN E. GIROUARD has been President and CEO of CAPITAL Asset Management Group, based in the Washington, DC metropolitan area, since 1984 and is the founder of the Institute for Financial Independence, which offers educational programs and other resources to individuals and corporations about financial goal-setting, planning, and investment.

He is a frequent speaker at industry and association meetings, and conducts classes at financial learning centers in Maryland and Delaware.

He has earned numerous industry awards and certifications, including Certified Financial Planner (CFP®), Certified Fund Specialist, Chartered Financial Consultant, Chartered Life Underwriter, Certified Senior Advisor, and Certified Estate Advisor. He is also licensed as a Conditionomics Coach™, showing couples how to integrate their financial plans with their personal goals, so they can achieve them sooner and safer.

He earned his BA in Economics from the University of Maryland at College Park and has been a member of the Board of the school's College Park Foundation, the Financial Committee of the Alumni Association, and the Board of the College of Behavioral and Social Sciences. He has also been active with the National Children's Center, Inc., a Washington, DC-based nonprofit providing services and opportunities to people with developmental disabilities.

Mr. Girouard lives in Washington, DC with his wife, Colleen, and two children, Caitlin and Coley.

Acknowledgments

A BOOK BECOMES WORDS ON PAPER only after a complex process, a long journey, and the help and encouragement of many others.

I am grateful to the thousands of clients who have passed through my doors, not only placing their financial futures in my hands, but also challenging me to test my ideas and helping me validate the concepts that are distilled here.

Many friends, family members, and colleagues read the manuscript in its various stages and offered thoughtful feedback that helped me refine the message. Among them were Jim and Herta Feely; Howard Offit; Sal Petruzzella; my parents, Gerry and Claire Girouard; and my in-laws, Jean and Jim Driscoll.

Special thanks go to Dan Sullivan, my long-term business coach, who helped me get past the obstacle of feeling overwhelmed by the idea of this project, and just take the first step toward making it a reality.

Brian O'Connell helped get this book out of my head and onto paper, and to stay focused during our weekly developmental conferences. Foster Winans, my editor, helped mold my thousands of words into a professional manuscript, and is responsible for helping develop the design, and shepherding the book through its production.

Special thanks go to my wife, Colleen, and our children, Caitlin and Coley, who made allowances in their lives and found patience in their hearts, so I could have the physical and mental space to see the job through.

Similarly, I want to acknowledge the people on whom I daily depend, the staff at Capital Asset Management Group who backed me up and kept the trains running on time when I was pre-occupied with the book: Michael Morgan, Rick Weinberg, Jennifer Bartley, Jennifer Edejer, Vernon Edejer, Dionne Cornelius, Rhonda Wintz, Karen Mclane, and Katrina Moody.

Preface

THE BOOK YOU HOLD IN YOUR HANDS is the distillation of a quarter century of experience helping rescue people from their misconceptions about how to achieve financial security. For all those years plus a few before that, when I was getting my education, I've listened to so-called Wall Street gurus spout the same flawed recommendations and tired investment bromides.

You've no doubt heard some and possibly all of the "keys to success" advocated by brokers and other investment-product salesmen, such as investing in index funds, betting on superior stock market returns, or sticking with mutual funds. Everyone claims to be—or have—an expert, and every firm claims it offers the best ideas. It can't be true, of course, but how can an ordinary person untangle all the hype and figure out what really is the best opportunity for them?

You're about to find out, as have my thousands of clients over the years. There is a better, more reliable way to create wealth. When you learn what it is, you may be surprised how much sense it makes, and understand how the investment marketing industry makes reaching your goals as frustrating and costly as possible.

The financial services industry is in the business of selling hope. It is unnecessary for the industry's success to produce results. Consequently, the investment industry—Wall Street, mutual fund companies, the bank with its CDs, the online trading houses, and so on—continues to peddle the same stale recipes for wealth creation that, when you really take a good hard look at them, were never good ideas to begin with. They rarely produce consistent returns for clients, but they do consistently make money for the industry.

I have helped my clients by going back to some basic truths about investments and money. I show them that by ignoring the Wall Street/investment industry noise, by thinking differently about the investment tools we've been given, they can create financial security for themselves and their families.

Among the lessons I hope you'll learn in these pages include that:

- Old-fashioned, participating whole life insurance provides all the key elements to guarantee financial success;

- Index investing may be the worst financial tool;
- The interest-only mortgage has been the best change in the mortgage industry in a long time;
- The stock market may average a 10 percent annual return, but people don't actually get 10 percent;
- Average rates of return are irrelevant in financial planning and may be the number one reason people's plans fail;
- Risk is not about the chance of losing money;
- 60 percent of individual wealth is eaten up by taxes, lost interest income, and unnecessary interest paid.

In the following pages, I'll reveal the inner workings of the investment industry, expose flaws and misconceptions in conventional wisdom, explain how those flaws keep you from your goals, and show you how real wealth is created, accumulated, and protected.

This is not a book about getting rich, it is about getting secure, about achieving financial independence, however you define it.

I invite you to read, learn, and prosper.

— JOHN E. GIROUARD
Washington, DC 2006

Introduction:
Ready for an Investor Makeover?

> *"Learning is like rowing upstream;*
> *not to advance is to drop back."*
> **—Old Chinese Proverb**

CHANCES ARE GOOD that you're reading this book because you're worried about your financial future. Chances are you should be.

According to some estimates, 95 percent of Americans are doomed to spend their retirement years mired in debt. Today's fast-food workforce of immigrants and youngsters is at risk of evolving into tomorrow's workforce of starving seniors spending their Golden Years shackled to the Golden Arches. All because they are afraid of change.

Baby boomers who think they have an inheritance coming and don't have to worry about retirement may be in for a shock. According to the AARP, because people are living longer, parents are more frequently having to spend down the money they'd planned on leaving to their families. Only one in seven boomers expects to inherit anything.

You may be one of the lucky ones who doesn't have to worry. But just in case you aren't, you hold in your hands a book that will show you how to make yourself over as an investor so that you will be able to live out your life in relative prosperity—just by thinking about money, and investing it, in new, creative ways based on time-proven concepts.

Change has always been the engine of progress and prosperity. History is replete with examples of how often greatness resides in those who have the courage and discipline to change the way they behave and think, to lead rather than follow.

Teddy Roosevelt was a weak, sickly child who was picked on so much he took up boxing and became a champion at it. He was also a lifelong learner—the pillow he died on had a book under it.

Clockwise from upper left: Michaelangelo, Thomas Edison, Teddy Roosevelt.

Thomas Edison authored 1,092 patents and was still exploring new ways of doing things at the age of eighty-three, when he was awarded his 1,093rd.

Michelangelo's favorite expression was, "I am still learning."

The spirit of change and vision are celebrated in medicine, industry, the military, fine arts—every corner of our culture.

Except in the investment industry, which I define as the industry that makes its money by shuffling yours around. In fact, its success depends on the absence of change, and on investor confusion. The investment industry considers the perfect customer to be one who meekly and gratefully hands over his wallet, asks no questions, and goes away, praying for good luck. And there are a lot of perfect customers.

The investment industry needs a serious makeover, but don't wait for it to happen. Investors need to give themselves makeovers—stop accepting poor results, start asking questions, learn that what they don't know IS hurting them, demand answers, and become informed and empowered. It's your money and you are responsible for what happens to it.

Each of us is born with the potential to create wealth. But nearly three decades as an investment professional have taught me that no one gets there by following the crowd. That's a serious problem when the crowd is as big as it's gotten in the past quarter century.

I've been challenging the system since the 1980s when I first went to work with a major insurance company, selling life insurance and pension products. When I had earned my degree as a professional financial planner, I believed that I had an obligation to my customers to recommend the best investments for their situation, not just what the insurance company wanted me to push.

So I did something that shocked my colleagues: I told my company that it was unethical

The investment industry considers the perfect customer to be one who meekly and gratefully hands over his wallet, asks no questions, and goes away, praying for good luck.

to force me to sell products that might not be in the best interests of my clients. I argued that I should have the right to sell products from other companies if I felt they were a better fit for a particular client's needs. I won my argument and ever since I have been developing my philosophy and approach from the unique perspective of someone who has had freedom of choice, but also a window into how the investment business really works.

I know firsthand how investment companies encourage their brokers and salespeople to sell you the "products" that yield the highest profit for the firm, or earn the biggest commission for the broker. As you read, you'll begin to understand that your goals have always taken second place to the fortunes of the firms whose products you are being encouraged to buy or invest in.

> *As you read, you'll begin to understand that your goals have always taken second place to the fortunes of the firms whose products you are being encouraged to buy or invest in.*

I also know, firsthand, what it's like to be worried about money. I grew up in central Connecticut, in a brand new post-World War II neighborhood of cookie-cutter homes. I was the youngest of four boys and my father was a small-town banker, which meant he earned a secure but middle-class income. It also meant he was conservative in the way children of the Depression tended to be: whatever we wanted, we had to work for it, even as kids.

My clothes came out of the hand-me-down barrel we kept in the basement. With three older brothers, I rarely wore anything new. I worked every summer— delivering newspapers, feeding pigs, busing tables—because I was expected to earn my parochial school and college fees, as well as the money to buy my first car AND pay the insurance premiums.

When he was about fifty years old, my father accepted a big promotion to become senior vice president of the largest bank in the state. Nine years later, just one year shy of his pension vesting, the bank was sold to a huge multi-national and he was out on the street. I'll never forget coming home from work that day and finding my parents in the kitchen, my mother weeping and my father with his head in his hands.

I reacted as any son might: I vowed to do whatever I could to help them regain their financial security. I learned early to be skeptical of large organizations and conventional thinking.

A few years later, having earned my investment advisor's credentials, I initiated a father-son discussion, roles reversed, about my parents' financial situation and my dad's retirement plans. He had a fifteen-year mortgage that he was striving to pay off by the time he turned seventy years old, the earliest he figured he could retire. He was paying an extra seven hundred dollars a month against the principal, and was worried that if he couldn't work for some reason, they'd have to make some unpleasant choices, like selling the house.

I got out my calculator and a pad and pencil and started doing some figuring. When I was done, I tore off the sheet of paper with my calculations and handed it to him. "Instead of paying off the mortgage early, give me the seven hundred dollars a month to invest," I said. "You start drawing Social Security—you're sixty-two now—and we'll make some other financial adjustments. That way, you can retire right now, today."

It took me a bit of explaining to convince him. He'd grown up in a culture that regarded debt as practically a sin, and thought that putting your money in the bank was the best way to create wealth.

In the end, he trusted me and went for it. Eight years later, for his seventieth birthday, I arranged a golf vacation with him to Ireland. At one point he reached in his pocket and presented me with a heavily creased piece of paper. It was the sheet on which I'd made his retirement calculations all those years before.

"We're exactly where you'd said we'd be," he told me with a confident, proud, and appreciative grin. Those are moments I live for and have been privileged to experience countless times.

You don't have to have grown up during the Depression, or been a conservative small-town banker, to be confused and misled by the roar of voices trying to get your attention. Our mailboxes overflow with glossy brochures, television seems wall-to-wall with investment industry ads, and newspapers and magazines are full of stories and advice warning about scams or touting the strategy-du-jour.

One of the most powerful tools in the Wall Street marketing arsenal is human nature. As more than one tyrant in history has observed, if you tell a lie big enough and often enough, people will come to believe it. One of the big investment lies, often believed by my new clients, is that if I just put their money in the stock market, they'll get a return of around 10 percent a year, practically guaranteed. You hear this everywhere, read it everywhere, and now it's assumed to be the truth.

You don't have to have grown up during the Depression, or been a conservative small-town banker, to be confused and misled by the roar of voices trying to get your attention.

That lie is statistical and significant. Compound annual return is not the same as compound interest you earn from your bank account. The math is completely different and returns are often misleading as a result.

Try this short quiz, and you'll see what I mean.

Bob had $100,000 in his IRA that he invested in a stock portfolio two years ago. Now he's at a cocktail party bragging that his portfolio has had an average annual return of 25 percent. You're impressed and you try to calculate in your mind what that comes to in dollars. Assuming he's telling the truth, what would you assume to be the value of Bob's IRA at the beginning of the third year?

Answers:

A. $156,250
B. $100,000
C. $150,000
D. $144,000
E. Any of the Above

Believe it or not, the answer could be any one of the above. Here's how that's possible.

Answer A—The one Bob wants you to believe:

Year one: $100,000 + 25% = $125,000
Year two: $125,000 + 25% = $156,250
Average: 25% + 25%/2 = 25% (assumes consistent compounding)

Answer B—When he only tells you about two years ago.

Year One: $100,000 + 100% = $200,000
Year Two: $200,000 - 50% = $100,000
Average: 100% - 50%/2 = 25% (considering volatility)

Answer C—The one he might admit to if challenged:

Year One: $100,000 + 50% = $150,000
Year Two: $150,000 + 0% = $150,000
Average: 50% + 0%/2 = 25% (without compounding)

Answer D—When he only tells you about the latest year:

Year One: $100,000 - 10% = $90,000
Year Two: $90,000 + 60% = $144,000
Average: -10% + 60%/2 = 25%

Numbers lie, and the investment industry throws numbers around like pixie dust, obscuring the ability of customers to distinguish between fact and fantasy. Articles in business magazines extol "The Ten Hottest Stocks" or "Seven Big Movers You Need to Add to Your Portfolio Now." Sizzle sells. Sadly, what sells is usually what investors should be avoiding.

> *Sizzle sells.*
>
> *Sadly, what sells is usually what investors should be avoiding.*

No one can predict the future, and some people who are supposed to be smart can't even tell the present. Alan Greenspan, the much-heralded former chairman of the Federal Reserve Board, said in 1990, "Those who argue that we are already in a recession…are reasonably certain to be wrong."

The problem was that the economy was already in recession but Greenspan—and most every other financial expert—didn't realize it yet. That's how difficult it is for anyone to figure out where the market, let alone the economy, is headed. Yet, people still flock to the so-called experts, and continue to give their money to mutual funds and other financial managers who claim they know something no one else does.

If that were true, then in The Wall Street Journal's regular "contest" between Wall Street's star money managers and a monkey with a dart, the money managers should win—but they don't. Time and again, the battle results in a draw, or the darts come out on top. That's not an investment strategy.

The point here is not to bash Wall Street or the rest of the investment complex, but to persuade you to ignore the hype, and get re-educated about how good investments work, and learn how they can work for your particular situation. I can't blame investors for being confused. I've been a financial advisor for twenty-five years and sometimes what's going on in the financial planning community confuses me, too.

The industry's leading lights can be counted on to say one thing one year and the opposite the next. Market timing? First they said it'll never work. Then Wall Street decided it was a great "new" idea. Asset allocation? The answer to our prayers—until a real bear market came around. Buy and hold? The true way to wealth—until the market tanks and what you're left holding is the bag.

The financial advisory industry is still relatively young and that helps explain some of the confusion and hyperbole. It is a competitive business and it's easier to attract potential

> *People scoff at astrologers and tarot card readers, but put on a suit and get a business card that says "stockbroker" on it, and people suddenly think you're an expert.*

clients with the hot, new idea and the fuzzy mathematics of average returns than to introduce them to dull but successful strategies like life insurance, a core of my investment approach. People scoff at astrologers and tarot card readers, but put on a suit and get a business card that says "stockbroker" on it, and people suddenly think you're an expert.

Investing and financial planning shouldn't be as complicated as it has become, or as risky. After years of outstanding returns and creating significant wealth for my clients—and myself—I've learned how to nurture money and make it grow consistently without experiencing the huge losses that most people suffered after the dot-com bubble.

When the financial industry isn't trying to sell us the latest hot idea, it encourages us to park our money in longer term certificates of deposit by offering a better rate so we can make more money. Mutual funds argue that by giving them our money and forgetting about it, it'll compound for years and we'll grow wealthy by doing nothing—just sit tight and accumulate. That's the exact opposite of what we should be doing.

In the following pages, you'll learn more about the myths propagated by Wall Street as facts, and why some of the simplest investment strategies are often the best. You may be surprised how easily worry can be turned into peace of mind.

PART I

The Ten Truths of
Wealth Creation

1 Ownership Drives Wealth

> *Upon the sacredness of property, civilization itself depends—the right of the laborer to his hundred dollars in the savings bank, and equally the right of the millionaire to his millions.*
> —Andrew Carnegie, founder of U.S. Steel

OWNERSHIP THAT IS BASED ON well-defined and legally-secure property rights is the foundation of prosperity, and it's what built America into a land of opportunity. As human beings, we are most motivated to care about what we own. It can even make the difference between life and death.

In Jamestown, Virginia—the first permanent English colony in what became the United States—the first two groups of settlers who tried to make a go of things basically starved to death. The leaders of those first two groups chose to organize the community into collective farms on which everyone worked and, regardless of how hard or smart they worked, every family received an equal share of food.

In his controversial 2004 book, "How Capitalism Saved America," author Thomas Dilorenzo argues that the first settlers failed because the lack of ownership and its potential reward undermined the settlers' work ethic. The third attempt to establish a permanent community was organized by a British governor named Sir Thomas Dale who imposed strict order and laws, including dividing up the arable land and establishing and enforcing property rights. The colony began to prosper as each family's yield from their labor determined how well their family was fed. Once people had control over their destinies, Jamestown could thrive and survive.

THE FOUR VEHICLES OF WEALTH

Many people confuse income with wealth, believing a large salary makes them rich. But wealth comes from ownership, and then only certain kinds of ownership. Wealth, for example, rarely comes from owning a car or a fancy wardrobe.

The creation of wealth is driven by four basic categories of ownership: ideas, real estate, stocks, and mutual life insurance societies.

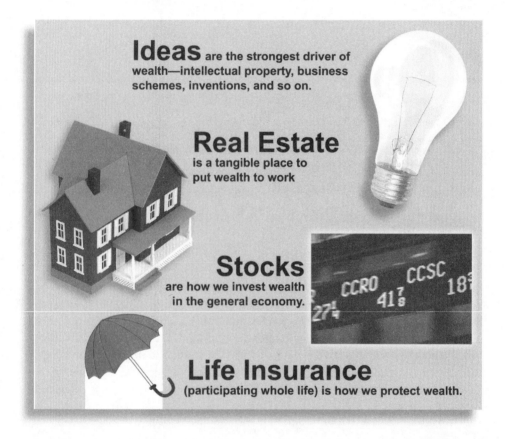

Ideas are the strongest driver of wealth—intellectual property, business schemes, inventions, and so on.

Real Estate is a tangible place to put wealth to work

Stocks are how we invest wealth in the general economy.

Life Insurance (participating whole life) is how we protect wealth.

In the pages and chapters ahead, I'll explain and give examples and illustrations of how, within each of the first three categories, there are basic decisions you can make that can increase the chances you'll achieve your goals. Some aspects of the ideas and approaches may be familiar to you, but if you're like most of my clients, you'll be surprised to discover how it all can work together for superior results. Like almost all my clients, you may be amazed to learn how valuable and important to wealth protection is an old vehicle we typically associate with our parents' generation: whole life insurance.

The guiding rule in creating wealth is control, but too much of what is recommended today in the form of investment products requires investors to surrender control. My experience has taught me ten truths about wealth creation, beginning with control:

The Ten Truths of Wealth Creation

1. The key to wealth is through ownership and control, not financial products.

2. The more money moves, the more wealth is created.

3. Everything in life has a cost and requires payments.

4. The biggest cost to wealth—up to 60 percent—is uncaptured interest income, unnecessary interest expense, and failure to manage taxes.

5. Rates of return and index investing as financial planning tools are misleading and meaningless.

6. Insurance is a contract, and understanding this concept is the key to creating and preserving wealth.

7. Risk is not about losing money.

8. Some debt is good, if you finance a thing no longer than its useful life.

9. The biggest obstacle to building wealth is the absence of reliable market information.

10. Financial independence begins with understanding and focusing on your life goals, as opposed to financial goals, and minimizing your future decisions.

OWNERSHIP AS A "NEW" OLD CONCEPT

More than any other nation on earth, America provides the opportunity and even the expectation for individuals to succeed. It was a founding principle of the nation, and our laws were written and interpreted to protect the rights and opportunities of the individual. Whether you failed or succeeded financially was considered a matter of character. If you succeeded, you had done so as a result of hard work and innovation. If you failed, it was your own shortcoming.

During the Depression years of the 1930s under President Franklin Roosevelt, the government established safety nets for those who'd been caught unprepared by the economic collapse. Over time, these grew to include programs such as Social Security, Medicaid and Medicare, food stamps, child tax credits, and so on.

Since the Reagan revolution of the 1980s, the pendulum has swung back toward personal rather than collective responsibility. Taxes and spending for social programs has diminished. Welfare was redefined and scaled back.

The trend toward personal responsibility and ownership principals has sparked an explosion of creativity, producing a seemingly limitless choice in financial vehicles and strategies. From a time when investment decisions were essentially limited to U.S. stocks and bonds, we've evolved a massive catalog of international investment vehicles that can be managed in an infinite number of strategies.

The trend toward personal responsibility and ownership principals has sparked an explosion of creativity, producing a seemingly limitless choice in financial vehicles and strategies.

It's even possible now to buy an investment product based on an index of real estate prices in individual cities. One could conceivably buy real estate in New York, and then hedge that investment with a real estate index investment that grows in value if New York real estate prices decline.

The problem with all these investment products is two-fold.

First, there are too many and they are too confusing for most people. Even if you had the time and the interest, you'd drive yourself crazy sorting through all the options and approaches. So most investors become easy targets for investment product sales people—brokers and investment advisors. Based on a recommendation, or a well-known firm, or something they may have read or seen on television, they tend to make choices out of hope and fear, but not out of confidence. This is not an investment strategy.

The second problem is that most of the investment products being offered lack an ownership element, my first Wealth Creation Truth. Even the most common forms of investment insurance being offered today do not give investors the control they need to build portfolios that will bring them financial independence. I will explain the ownership paradox in detail in later sections. For now, it is important to understand the role of ownership in wealth creation.

Ownership induces people to act responsibly. As the Greek philosopher Aristotle noted, "What belongs in common to the most people is accorded the least care." For instance, when was the last time you washed a rental car?

Without ownership of printing presses, paper, and ink, there would be no free press. Without ownership of land and buildings, there would be no freedom of association, no freedom of common worship, no freedom of action in general.

A free society is an ownership society, which is why capitalism has flourished in Western cultures, but failed everywhere else.

The success of American capitalism is not a result of some special money gene in our DNA. If it were, islands of prosperity like Hong Kong and Taiwan would not have existed. The Chinese are excellent, ambitious businesspeople anywhere they find freedom and legal protection of ownership rights. Even under the glacial improvements in ownership rights in the Peoples Republic of China in the past twenty-five years, the Chinese are proving themselves just as competitive, aggressive, and innovative as the best in the US.

Ownership makes markets possible, and markets make reliable pricing possible, which allows us to capture a portion of the additional value our energies and investments create. Without the prices made possible by the exchange of property rights in free markets, there are no signals to guide entrepreneurs to the best use of resources or to coordinate the efforts of large numbers of people and resources.

It would seem as if a true ownership society is just around the corner in America. Home ownership is at an historic high, seventy percent of households according to the US Census Bureau. Roughly half of households own stock.

...even as Americans were gaining ownership, they were losing wealth.

But even as Americans were gaining ownership, they were losing wealth. Between 1983 and 1998, government statistics reported that the bottom forty percent of households by income suffered a 76 percent decrease in net worth. The problem is they were trying to own too much of the wrong things, and using credit cards to do it.

A majority of Americans are drowning in expensive credit card debt. Between 1989 and 2001, the average household more than doubled its credit card debt, with the poorest families recording the largest rise. Personal bankruptcies in 2003—at the end of a recession—were nearly double the number in 1994, the end of an earlier recession.

For a time, the news was full of stories about how some homeowners had scored windfalls from spiking real estate prices. But, US homeowners on average have a lower debt-to-equity ratio in their homes than at nearly any point during the past half century. Homeowners have been spending their equity for living and luxuries.

Half of households may own stock, but 40 percent of those own less than $5,000 worth of

The problem is they were trying to own too much of the wrong things, and using credit cards to do it.

equities, typically in defined contribution 401(k) pension plans. This is not true ownership. Unlike the guaranteed pensions of the past, these plans shift investment risk onto employees. Life in this corner of the ownership society can be grim—total return on the S&P 500 index for the past five years has been minus 2.2 percent. So much for just putting your money in the stock market and watching it go up 10 percent a year.

GOOD AND BAD NEWS FOR U.S. COMPETITIVENESS

When it comes to the wealth imbedded in ideas, America is the most innovative nation on earth.

- We generate the most patents per capita, one per three thousand Americans versus four thousand for the Japanese, six thousand for the Taiwanese, and ten million for the Chinese.

- We conduct more research and development than any other nation. The United States funds 44 percent of the total worldwide investment in research and development. That's equal to the combined total of Japan, the United Kingdom, Canada, France, Germany, and Italy.

- American scientific output is greater, as measured by scientific publications per million population, than Europe and Japan.

- Our labs and universities remain the most attractive destination for the best and brightest young minds in the world. Eight-five percent of the PhDs who come here from China stay because it's a better place to live and do business.

- Our culture richly rewards risk-taking, encourages entrepreneurship, and celebrates success.

- And of greatest significance today, Americans are protected by the most rational, predictable, and transparent framework for intellectual property rights in the world, encouraging investment and inciting innovation.

To put this in perspective, consider that high-ranking Chinese officials regard the lack of protection of intellectual property rights a greater threat to their own economy than to ours. Right now, China's economy is based on the supply of cheap labor to the world. With that nation's economy growing rapidly, it will one day lose that advantage and unless Chinese entrepreneurs can be certain they can be rewarded for their efforts, China could suffer an economic implosion from lack of home-grown innovation.

America is changing from a consumer and manufacturing economy into a market economy, where the creation of new ideas and intellectual property generates the highest returns. We create the idea, own the idea, and others manufacture the finished product.

Wealth is in the ownership of the idea.

THE RULE OF LAW AS RULE OF THUMB

To create economic growth and wealth from ideas takes investment capital and an appetite for risk. But before anyone commits investment capital, investors need secure property rights and the force of law to uphold them. Property rights are the rules of ownership, use, and transference.

Private ownership encourages property improvement. Anyone who has ever been a landlord knows that renters have no incentive to maintain or increase the value of your property.

The same is true in business. With secure ownership of assets, we can borrow against those assets to start businesses and create prosperity. If you own your business instead of working for wages, you'll put in as many hours as it takes to make it a success. Wherever freedom is uncertain and ownership is not guaranteed, banks won't lend against assets, business creation is stifled, wealth cannot be captured.

Wherever freedom is uncertain and ownership is not guaranteed, banks won't lend against assets, business creation is stifled, wealth cannot be captured.

Secure property rights make life easier for the poorest nations, and opens up opportunities for all, not just the rich. Hernando de Soto, a world-celebrated Peruvian economist, wrote a ground-breaking book on this subject: "The Mystery of Capital." In it he illustrates just how much of the world's wealth lies fallow:

"If we extend property rights to all real estate held but not legally owned by the poor of the Third World and former communist nations, it would approach $9.3 trillion. This is about twice the total circulated U.S. money supply. It is nearly the value of all the companies listed on the main stock exchanges of the world's twenty most developed countries."

THE GLOBAL WAR OVER IDEAS

In every corner of the globe, battles are being fought over the wealth imbedded in ideas. And it has to do with much more than bootleg movies on the streets of Beijing or Jakarta. The battles illustrate in stark terms why capitalism and wealth creation flourishes here, and struggles elsewhere.

How strongly American laws protect ownership of wealth was illustrated in the Blackberry case of 2006 when the courts almost put out of business an entire communications network on which thousands of businesses and millions of people relied every day. The reason: copyright infringement.

In another US courtroom, the music industry managed to derail Internet portal Napster from letting its members swap digital music files without compensating the publishers and musicians. Napster's file-sharing technology was found to violate copyrights.

Contrast those examples with what has happened in other parts of the world.

Global pharmaceutical firms went to court in recent years to challenge a South African law that permitted the manufacture and importation of generic AIDS drugs. When the companies' defense of their patent rights became a public relations fiasco, the case was quickly dropped. South Africa's health minister later called the high prices for lifesaving medicines a "crime against humanity." The predictable result: fewer life-saving medicines were available to South Africans.

Across the Atlantic, in "democratic" Europe, there is a credible and gaining movement toward a policy called "software libre," giving preferences in government procurement to software that can be freely copied and distributed. The Euro Linux Alliance argues that only free software "preserves privacy, individual liberties, and the right for every citizen to access public information." If they succeed, slumping Europe will have an even harder time than it already has trying to keep up with the rest of the world.

The scope of these controversies is vast and touches virtually every aspect of life: ownership of the formula for an aids vaccine; a Miles Davis riff; a software algorithm; a new way to uncork a wine bottle.

There are three main causes for this war over ideas.

First, brainpower drives the modern economy. There are more demands to own ideas and more demands for cheaper access to ideas. Second, technological change has made it harder to protect ideas. More people want to use technology to get access to intellectual property. Third, globalization has made it easier for intellectual property to spread to parts of the world with weaker protection of ideas.

In a variant on Gresham's Law—bad money drives out good money—a nation that fails to protect patents drives down global standards, making it harder to enforce ownership rights everywhere.

There are important lessons in all this for building a model for financial independence. We want to avoid tying up our wealth in ideas over which we lack control.

In a variant on Gresham's Law—bad money drives out good money—a nation that fails to protect patents drives down global standards, making it harder to enforce ownership rights everywhere.

THE SOCIAL STAIRCASE OF REAL ESTATE

As Hernando de Soto noted, one of the greatest benefits of Western economies is the long-held right to own property. Contrast this with Egypt where 92 percent of all buildings and land are owned outside the legal property system, without recognized title deeds. The same holds true of businesses. Egyptians cannot benefit financially from ownership of most of their land and businesses, which has played havoc with their economy for decades.

Very few African countries grant citizens property titles. Instead, property remains in the hands of the state or, often, its corrupt leaders. No surprise, then, that Africa has struggled with stunted development and economic growth.

Contrast that with the US, where the Homestead Act of 1862, considered one of the most important pieces of legislation in our nation's history, turned over vast amounts of government land to private citizens as long as they were willing to live on and work it. The Homestead Act became the foundation of modern principles of legal ownership and development of property, and helped define real estate ownership as the primary staircase to social growth.

Everyone knows how much wealth was created during the recent housing market bubble. What made it so extraordinary was the rapid rise in prices over a short period of time. These bubble markets never last, and the historic profits cannot be counted on as part of an investment strategy.

...bubble markets never last, and the historic profits cannot be counted on as part of an investment strategy.

However, real estate will always be a financial vehicle because an investor can own a piece of property using someone else's money. This leveraging is so fundamental to our economy that it is one of the few segments financed in part by the government through interest deductions.

The spirit of the Homestead Act remains alive and well, and examples abound, like Martha S., a client who had a solid, substantial income working as a programmer for a division of IBM—until the division was sold out from under her. Bahamian-born of Haitian descent, she decided to try to build her assets with real estate. She already owned her residence, a town house in Tampa.

Through a program for first-time investors, she got one hundred percent financing on the purchase of a two-bedroom condo she could rent out. Then she bought another rental condo near the Walt Disney Resort in Orlando, using her savings for the down payment. She had followed the first two Wealth Creation Truths—ownership and control, and she kept her money moving.

TAKING STOCK, TAKING OWNERSHIP

Ideas and real estate are wealth creators, but for those who aren't interested in inventing or creating intellectual property, or want more than real estate offers, we have equity ownership—shares of stock. Here the decisions become complex, and I explore them in detail in Chapters Nine and Ten.

An investor becomes an owner when he or she purchases a share of stock, even though the piece of paper on which the certificate is printed has no intrinsic value, nor does it guarantee future value. The issuer of the stock does not guarantee a return, but they do transfer to the buyer an equal portion of the risk in exchange for a chance to secure an equal portion of the company's profit, in the form of dividends and/or appreciation in the price of the stock. Stock ownership is the only investment that can be held in multiple formats (a retirement account for example) while retaining the single truly capitalist characteristic of ownership.

LIFE INSURANCE AS PROTECTION AND OWNERSHIP

The problem with most insurance products being offered today is that they deny you ownership and control. In most cases, your money is put to work enriching the shareholders of the insurance company.

Using the three different vehicles—ideas, real estate, and equity stocks—an investor will build more or less wealth, depending on his or her choices. The fourth component, insurance, is complex and confusing even for most investment professionals. Insurance is intended to provide the wealth you've created with safety through ownership.

It's not quite your parent's life insurance, but it's also not the plethora of insurance products being peddled today by the investment industry. That's why I have chosen to devote several chapters to making it clear. You can jump directly to Chapters Sixteen through Nineteen to find out more now.

The problem with most insurance products being offered today is that they deny you ownership and control. In most cases, your money is put to work enriching the shareholders of the insurance company. Why not own the insurance company, too? That's the way it used to be, when the majority of insurance policies were issued by "mutual" insurance companies, in which the policy-holders were also owners. The old system worked so well that, during the Great Depression while bank customers and stock investors lost their shirts, mutual insurance company policies kept their values, preserving the wealth of their policyholder/owners.

The good news is that mutual, or what we now call participating, insurance companies still exist, although it takes some research to find the best ones.

But what, you may be asking yourself, about bonds and bank certificates of deposit as safe ways to preserve wealth? These are not ownership vehicles. A bond is evidence that you lent money, to the government, corporation, or other entity. Outside of government, you are typically lending money to someone who will use it to enhance their own wealth through ownership.

You earn interest, but you do not otherwise participate in the benefit your money generates. A certificate of deposit is evidence that you lent money to the bank, which turns around and lends it out at tremendous leverage—for every dollar you lend the bank, the bank earns interest income on ten.

This is not ownership, and the return never compensates for the loss due to taxes and the erosion of inflation. Nobody builds wealth just by lending money.

THE BIG PICTURE

Everything about life is cyclical and no one can guarantee consistent results. For example, I like to remind clients that two to three times per decade they can expect to see their assets in the stock market go down instead of up. Once in a while there will be a big pothole. But all financial assets grow in a saw-tooth manner. It is a constant process of advancing and pulling back.

People have their own cycles, as well as their own world views. Some people worry constantly, even after they've got more money than they'll ever need in a lifetime. Some people are never satisfied. A very successful Wall Street executive retired from his business with a $600 million payout. His estate lawyer asked him how he intended to spend his retirement. He replied, straight-faced, "I'd like to see if now I can make some real money."

The key is to focus on long-term results. As a media-driven culture, we've become obsessed with the instantaneous, pouncing on hot trends or reacting to panics that whipsaw people's emotions and encourage thoughtless or poorly executed financial decisions. That's why the tenth Wealth Creation Truth should probably be the first: **"Financial independence begins with understanding and focusing on your life goals—as opposed to financial goals—and minimizing your future decisions."**

Emotions should never guide your financial decisions. It was emotion that drove my father to believe he'd have to work eight more years just to be able to retire at seventy years old. Instead, I showed him through common sense and my understanding of him that he didn't have to wait.

Since we are each responsible for our choices, they should be made with self-knowledge and common sense. Your financial choices should allow you to live your life with minimal anxiety about the future, able to ignore the investment industry noise. In the following chapters I will explain how all the pieces of this puzzle work, how they fit together, and how you can use this knowledge to create your own financially independent future.

2 Why You Shouldn't Bank on Banks

> *If you borrow a thousand dollars, the bank owns you. If you borrow a million, you own the bank.*
>
> —Economist John Maynard Keyes (paraphrased)

IN THE WANING YEARS OF THE 1980S, a huge scandal erupted in the once staid but newly-deregulated savings and loan industry involving banks in Texas and California whose officers and directors made spectacularly bad and callously corrupt real estate loans. The scandal came to light as real estate prices collapsed. More than four hundred bankers ended up with criminal records, and the US government had to step in with hundreds of billions in tax dollars to bail the financial system out of its mess.

From this cataclysm a new proverb entered the language of finance, poached from a line in "The Three Penny Opera:" the easiest way to rob a bank is to own one.

Nearly two decades later, aspects of history may be repeating themselves. As I write this, the real estate market is beginning to unravel after an extended bull run. Hopefully, this time the downturn won't threaten to take the rest of the economy with it.

Even if it does, one thing will remain constant–owning a bank is a great way to make money, even for honest people. So unless you happen to own one, you should be putting your money to work someplace else, where you are the owner.

Once you understand how banks work, you'll be able to make better-informed financial choices and avoid letting others profit from using your property. You'll understand why paying extra principal on your home mortgage is the same as loaning money to the bank money at zero percent interest. Sounds counter-intuitive, but I'm going to prove it to you.

THE MATH OF BANKING

Owning a bank is so profitable that in the first five years of the new millennium, more than seven hundred new ones opened their doors in the US, many with multiple branches. That explains why you've seen them sprouting on every corner like convenience stores. Who knew we had such a shortage of bank branches? Add to that Internet-based accounts, and we are awash in places to stash your cash.

More banks are fighting for your money because they know what you are learning in this book about the second Wealth Creation Truth: the more money moves, the more wealth is created.

More banks are fighting for your money because they know what you are learning in this book about the second Wealth Creation Truth: the more money moves, the more wealth is created. Banks make money when yours moves around, and the frequency with which money moves through our economic system has accelerated. ATMs are everywhere, the principal way we obtain currency. Who cashes a check anymore? Bank debit and credit cards are becoming the principal way we spend money.

Investment horizons are shorter—we buy real estate and flip it, we day-trade, we badger public companies to produce consistent high growth. Technology makes it easy for money to chase the best return, seamlessly and globally. Almost every day a new investment vehicle is invented. We've just been through two historic speculative periods, back-to-back: the stock market and then real estate. Our money has been flying around our economy.

All this liquidity is a good thing for our financial system. Before the 1980s explosion in the financial markets, it was harder to unlock the value in certain assets, and to diversify in such a way as to both unlock value and protect against downturns. It's interesting to note that we seem to have had fewer financial crises than we did in the past, serious meltdowns when the government had to step in to save the system, as happened during the savings and loan disaster of the early 1990s, and in 1998 when a global currency collapse took down some very large investment operations. In spite of terrorism and high commodity prices, the ease with which money moves seems to have helped dampen shocks to the financial system. Today, money moves in a heart-beat, and we have at our fingertips a nearly bottomless box of tools to take advantage of opportunities almost anywhere at almost any hour of the day.

Every time all this money moves, banks harvest some of it, in direct fees, hidden costs, or unpaid interest—or all three. It's death by a thousand cuts. Banks make money by lending each of your dollars–from your CDs, IRAs, or other cash deposits–to as many as ten different borrowers, collecting fees or interest from all of them. Bankers, the old joke goes, follow the 3-6-3 rule: pay 3 percent interest on deposits, charge 6 percent on loans, and head to the golf course at three o'clock.

Mortgage banks earn the bulk of their profits from the fees they charge for arranging your loan. There's so much money to be made that they often immediately turn around and sell their loans, and its income, to other banks. They are all making money using your assets. If this makes no sense to you, you're on the right track.

Banks and their services or products overwhelm many consumers because there is so much more to grasp in order to make a smart choice. There are too many options, too much marketing hype, and not enough information to figure out which, if any, are good for you. Life, and money, shouldn't be that complicated.

Banks provide three basic services.

- Banks are a safe place to keep money. A bank, which gets its charter from the government and insurance against loss for the bulk of your deposits, is designed to be financially solid.

- Banks provide a safe, guaranteed way to transfer funds, by writing a check, by phone, by computer, or automatic deductions.

- Banks loan your money, through regular loans and mortgages, or through credit cards. They "buy" or get deposits by paying interest to get you to lend it to them, then turn around and "sell" your money, or lend it out, at higher rates.

DO AS BANKS DO, NOT AS THEY SAY

Banks tell us that the longer we leave our money in them—in certificates of deposit, mutual funds, and so on—the more money we'll have when we need it. Then they turn around and accelerate the movement of our money by investing in opportunities that earn them more than they're paying us. While banks are encouraging us to allow our money to accumulate in their fire-proof vaults and insured accounts, they do the opposite for themselves.

Instead, we should be doing what the bank does—accelerating our money and capturing the additional interest and other income now being earned on your money by the bank. In order to

While banks are encouraging us to allow our money to accumulate in their fire-proof vaults and insured accounts, they do the opposite for themselves.

reach your money goals sooner and safer, you have to gain more control over, and ownership of, your money.

"A banker," Mark Twain quipped a century ago, "is a fellow who lends you his umbrella when the sun is shining and wants it back the minute it begins to rain." The same concept underlies the banker's favorite question of the loan applicant, "Got any collateral?" It's rare for a bank to lend without it, which is one reason why banks are safe places to stash your bankroll. They will lend you money, but only if you are willing to give up control of an asset of similar value—a home, a stock portfolio, and so on.

Before the Homestead Act helped define real estate as collateral for loans, credit was typically on the barter system or through mutual societies, precursors to today's credit unions. Banks then began to lend on a more speculative basis—lending a merchant money against an expected shipment from aboard, if the vessel didn't sink; to a farmer against his expected crop, if a drought or flood didn't destroy it; to a stock speculator against his expected trading profit, unless he was wrong and got wiped out. There was more risk and more and bigger financial disasters.

You don't have to be a Morgan or a Carnegie to take advantage of the first two Wealth Creation Truths: wealth comes through ownership and control, and from the movement of money.

The challenge was to figure out how to lend in such a way as to make the borrower assume all the risk. The way to do that was through collateralization—if you failed to repay a loan, you stood to lose assets of roughly equal or greater value.

Banks don't play by the same rules. The Federal Reserve Bank, which governs the banking business, requires as little as three percent of a bank's assets to be held in actual cash reserves. That means that for every dollar you lend the bank, in return for a very low interest rate, the bank can lend, and earn interest on, many dollars. That simple math explains why some of the wealthiest people in the world—legendary financiers such as J.P. Morgan, Andrew Carnegie, and Andrew W. Mellon—owned banks.

You don't have to be a Morgan or a Carnegie to take advantage of the first two Wealth Creation Truths: wealth comes through ownership and control, and from the movement of money. The next step is to give you an example of how it works in practice.

3 The Ownership Paradox

> *Those who hold and those who are without property have...distinct interests in society.*
> —James Madison, "Father" of the U.S. Constitution

AS SOMEONE WHO GREW UP wearing hand-me-downs, and expected to work to pay my way through parochial school and college, I've made a special effort to try to instill in my children a healthy respect and intelligent attitude about money. One day my twelve-year-old son and I had stopped for a bite to eat when I saw an opportunity to teach him a basic lesson about money and wealth creation. We were sitting in the restaurant and I asked him to identify the three categories of people represented there. He needed a little coaching so I pointed out that we were part of one group—the consumer.

"Okay, what about the cook who prepared the food, and the person who took our order and brought it to us?" I asked.

"They work here. They're employees, right?"

"Right. That's two. Who's left?"

He got stuck. I prodded. "Where does the money go that we pay?"

"The waitress takes it."

"And then what happens?"

"She gives it to her boss."

"And then?"

The power of ownership is such a basic concept that even a child instinctively gets it.

Eventually he figured out that the third group was the restaurant owner.

"Which one would you rather be—consumer, employee, or owner?"

"The owner, of course!"

The power of ownership is such a basic concept that even a child instinctively gets it.

We all have a choice in life: to be a consumer, employee, or owner. To tip the scales of your financial affairs in your favor, you should always try to consume the products and services you purchase from firms in which you are also, in some fashion, an owner. That doesn't mean you have to buy a restaurant in order to enjoy a meal away from home. It does, however, suggest a smart investment approach, not unlike buying stock in the power company that supplies your electricity.

The Ownership Paradox poses this dilemma: how does one become an owner and a consumer at the same time? The answer is by paying a cost. If you want a future guarantee of financial peace of mind, you have to be prepared to pay for it, assuming the benefit will exceed the cost and risk.

One of the characteristics that make our economy unique and elegant is that it is relatively easy—easier than any other place on the planet—to become an owner. As I explained to my son, we could skip a few of our trips to the restaurant in which we were functioning solely as consumers and use the money we saved to buy a share of the restaurant company's stock, thereby becoming an owner. Then, everything we consume in that restaurant is not only nutritious and tasty, but it's also putting money in our pockets.

In practical terms, that's at the core of what is meant by an "ownership society," an intriguing but poorly understood concept. What does it really mean? For one thing, it means that individuals take better care of things they own. As the Greek philosopher Aristotle wrote, "What belongs in common to the most people is accorded the least care: they take thought for their own things above all."

Just as home ownership creates responsible homeowners, widespread ownership of other assets creates responsible citizens. Vaclàv Klaus, prime minister of the newly capitalistic Czech Republic from 1992 until 1997, pointed out the disastrous effect of government control of private property during the communist years: "The worst environmental damage occurs in countries without private property, markets, or prices." He was speaking about Eastern Europe, but the same applies to China, an environmental

> *As the Greek philosopher Aristotle wrote, "What belongs in common to the most people is accorded the least care: they take thought for their own things above all."*

disaster area, and any other nation where ownership is not a fundamental right.

Owners feel dignity, pride, and confidence. They have a stake in more than their own property, but also in their community and their society. There's nothing particularly noble about this instinct. It remains an ownership motivation. If you own a house, its value—your wealth—will depend on good public safety, clean streets, highly-rated schools, and so on.

The United States has the most widespread property ownership in history, nearly seventy percent in 2006. About half of households own, directly or through IRAs and other vehicles, shares of stock. That's up from about twenty percent in 1983. That means almost half of Americans directly benefited from the long bull market trend that ran from 1982 to 2000.

The best way to create an ownership society is to give more people the opportunity to become capitalists.

But half of Americans are not owners. The best way to create an ownership society is to give more people the opportunity to become capitalists. And the way to do that is more obvious and possible than most people believe. The key is insurance.

In addition to ordinary life insurance that provides a cash benefit when a person dies, insurance companies also sell what are called annuities, policies that provide a stream of payments, and are regulated by government as insurance. Annuities and pensions that pay a benefit for life are, in effect, insurance against outliving your financial resources. Some life insurance contracts accumulate cash values, which can be withdrawn or borrowed against and some are financial instruments used to accumulate or liquidate wealth.

Mutual companies are owned by policyholders, which is why we refer to the policies they sell as "participating."

Insurance used to be the ugly step-sister of the financial services industry. Most insurance companies were mutual entities that shared risk with their customer-owners, looking after the less fortunate, and keeping a customer's money safe so it would be there for retirement.

Insurance companies were expected to be prudent in managing their customer's money by minimizing risk and expenses while growing the value of customers' insurance contracts. By efficiently running their businesses, these old-fashioned mutual insurance companies could offer a reasonable, if unglamorous, guarantee. These contracts are still the only financial ownership vehicle that provide a guarantee, with certain other benefits that are described in detail in Chapters Sixteen through Nineteen.

Mutual companies are owned by policy-holders, which is why we refer to the policies they sell as "participating." They exist to serve the insurance needs of their policyholders at reasonable prices, to protect the interests of all policyholders, and if run efficiently, can pay dividends to their policyholders.

These mutual insurance contracts were once the standard in the industry, but in the past decade there has been a broad movement to convert mutually-owned insurance companies to companies owned by stockholders. Investors, who may have no other connection with the company, expect to receive a profit from their investment. A stock insurance company works for its stockholders and is obligated to do what's best for them. Policyholders come second, because they are not owners. They are merely customers.

A stock insurance company works for its stockholders and is obligated to do what's best for them. Policyholders come second, because they are not owners. They are merely customers.

The simplest way to describe the difference between the two is that stock-owned companies offer lower-priced, higher-risk products, and mutual firms offer higher-priced, lower-risk products. For the purposes of wealth creation, the biggest difference is that participating life insurance from a mutual insurance company solves the ownership paradox. You own the company that sells you the product.

Today, less than 20 percent of insurance companies are mutual holding companies. The rest of the industry has switched to stock, and they reward their shareholders by offering you a dizzying array of insurance products that may or may not suit your needs but generate a profit for the company.

Today's typical insurance companies are more like stock investment players and have become a major force in the financial services market. They sell products, not guarantees. The shift in the insurance industry from policy-holder as owner to policy-holder as a wealth-conscious consumer is a great example of the Ownership Paradox.

PART II

Wealth Creation Boot Camp— Setting Goals and Strategies

4 The Seven Keys to Financial Growth

HOW WE CREATED A WEALTH OF OPPORTUNITY

There has never been a better time for the average investor who wants to create wealth. That is an enormous change from the past. Since the inception of the financial markets in the mid-1800s until the last two decades, the individual investor was at the end of the food chain, prey for powerful investors who controlled the financial markets. Banks, insurance companies, pension funds, and other powerhouses ran the game and set the rules.

The retirement savings of the middle class were often concentrated in employer pension funds, the guarantee of Social Security, and "rainy day" savings accounts. Stock trading was dominated by the wealthy.

That began to change in the 1970s when price-fixing in brokerage commissions ended and the cost of trading came down. In the 1980s, after nearly fifteen years of poor stock market performance, hyper-inflation, high interest rates, political scandals, and recessions, the stock market exploded. With the advent of computer networks to transmit price information rapidly, and cable television to broadcast business news, suddenly the man on the street had access to much of the same information as the people working in the investment business.

Meanwhile, industrial America was going down the drain and taking along with it the lifetime jobs and the pension guarantees that working people had come to rely on for retirement. Social Security began to look shaky. The Reagan Revolution reintroduced the idea of more personal responsibility and less social promise.

For those with savings or other funds, high interest rates meant it had been easy to make a lot of money with no risk by buying the safest investment—government bonds. People had been spoiled by those huge returns and when interest rates declined in the 1980s, everyone began to look for other investments to replace them.

The stock market took off, and the public piled in. Savers became investors, mutual funds sprung up on every corner, and the entire financial services industry began a two-decades long evolution into the global supermarket of ideas, products, and strategies that we have today.

In 1960 there were 160 mutual funds with assets of $105 billion in current dollars (including the effect of inflation). In 2005, the Investment Company Institute—an industry group—reported 8,000 mutual funds, with assets of about $8 trillion, a 75-fold increase in twenty-five years.

...with all this opportunity—widespread information, lots of choices, and the speed with which money can move—why aren't more Americans getting rich in the financial markets?

Much of the expansion was fueled by retirement accounts as employers shifted away from costly defined benefit plans to defined contribution plans, like the 401(k), which give employees more control, and more responsibility.

The end result of all this has been a revolution in individual investing, offering a wealth of opportunities. But with all this opportunity—widespread information, lots of choices, and the speed with which money can move—why aren't more Americans getting rich in the financial markets?

For most people, the stock market remains an impenetrable maze. For insiders, it remains an uneven playing field, in their favor. In one fashion or another, they continue to have access to what's happening in the business world ahead of their customers, giving them the chance to get out of bad positions and into lucrative ones long before individual investors.

Wall Street insiders also get better access to low-risk, high-profit deals. For example, some investor advocates report that, in spite of well-publicized scandals, the largest institutional investors are still reaping the lion's share of profits from initial public offerings (IPOs).

You can't create wealth by complaining, but you can by understanding how the system works, and learning where the real opportunities are.

> *You can't create wealth by complaining, but you can by understanding how the system works, and learning where the real opportunities are.*

THE PURPOSE OF MONEY IN YOUR LIFE

Ours is a success-obsessed culture, as evidenced by the endless supply of money and self-help books that become best-sellers. Yet many of the people I meet are lost when it comes to defining their life dreams. They will tell me they need a certain amount of money to retire. The favorite number these days is $1 million, but everyone has a different lifestyle, and different expectations and perceptions. Some think that if they can just pay off their home mortgage, and be able to enjoy a few vacations each year, they'll be set for the rest of their lives. For others, $600 million is a starting point.

The common denominator is the desire for freedom from want, and the freedom to choose. The problem is there is too much choice, and too much chatter. We seem to have an unlimited number of investments tools, and no way to discern which is right for us. We're bombarded from every side by advice, opinions, warnings, tips, and so on from family, friends, the media, and the salespeople peddling their investment products.

MISLEADING INVESTMENT CLICHÉS

No load funds are better than load funds.
Insurance is a great investment.
Compound interest is your friend.
The stock market return averages **10 percent a year**.
Stocks always do better than bonds.
Paying cash is the secret to wealth.
Fees and expenses are the most important factor in determining return.
First **pay off** your home mortgage.
Forget **Social Security**.
Subtract your age from 100 to get the percentage of your portfolio that should be in stocks.
Index investing is better than active management.
The economy is **good**.
The economy is **bad**.

Some of these sound like they make sense, and some sound like nonsense. Either way, none of them say anything about your personal financial wealth and well being.

Consider the question that ranks second only to "How's the weather?" How do you think the economy's doing? The answer usually determines whether we feel confident or fearful, and those emotions often produce self-fulfilling results. If the media hammers long enough on how real estate prices are stabilizing and how bad it's going to be when housing prices collapse, you're likely to either feel fearful and sell, or hold on and pull back on your other spending. Either way, you're helping to fulfill the prophesy.

There's always the possibility of a true global financial disaster some day, but it's helpful to remember that even in the depths of the Great Depression fortunes were made, and preserved. Even after hundreds of banks collapsed in the wake of the savings-and-loan scandals in the early 1990s, we shook ourselves off and produced the most powerful bull market in history. Even in the wake of the financial crash triggered by the terrorist attacks of 9/11, the financial system chugged along and since then, a great deal of wealth has been created.

The perceived state of the economy is a distraction from the more important question: what do you want from the rest of your life?

The perceived state of the economy is a distraction from the more important question: what do you want from the rest of your life? A discussion about wealth should be about your personal and professional goals and dreams. Financial goals should not drive your life choices. It should be the other way around. But it rarely is.

If a client tells me she wants to have a million dollars saved by the time she's fifty, I ask "What for?" If a client tells me his goal is to pay off the home mortgage, I ask, "Why? Are you planning to die in it?"

Your goals, based on your values, should determine how much money you'll need to reach them. Too often, people focus on objectives without taking into account what really matters. Social scientists have identified three levels of values that should be part of any discussion about financial goals. Level one is the lower self: money to pay bills and feel secure. Level two is how you feel toward others.

Level three is the higher self, loosely defined as the meaning of life, which includes faith and feelings of destiny.

In my financial advisory practice I have identified seven primary roles that money plays in almost everyone's life. Each can have different values.

The Seven Roles of Money

1. FAMILY: spouse, children, parents, grandchildren, extended family.

2. HEALTH: maintenance, special needs, continuing care.

3. COMMUNITY: where we live, work, schools, where we wish to retire.

4. CHARITIES: which ones matter to us.

5. LEISURE: travel and entertainment.

6. TANGIBLE ASSETS: such as a home.

7. PROFESSIONAL: what we want to do after we retire.

PERSONAL AND PROFESSIONAL GOALS BEFORE FINANCIAL

It's a myth, perpetuated by the media and the investment industry, that wealth is created in the financial markets. The truly wealthy got there through exploitation of ideas or working hard and smart at their professions. The financial services industry's role is to preserve and protect the wealth that people create in their personal and professional careers.

The primary conflict in wealth creation is between what the financial industry wants us to believe—that we need to invest more and spend less—and the economic freedom we seek in our financial lives. If you can't make sacrifices, we are persuaded that we must invest more aggressively, and take on more risk.

The real reason people don't retire when they'd like to is lack of confidence. That's what held my father back, when he thought he needed to work until he was seventy years old, and made his primary goal to pay off his mortgage. Once I was able to demonstrate a different approach, he had the confidence to relax and enjoy the fruits of his labors.

When people approach wealth creation with the same dedication and confidence they have about their families and careers, they have a better chance of achieving their objectives. The courage and motivation to make good decisions begins with a discussion of your values.

5 How Much Is Enough?

> **Money is a good servant but a bad master.**
> —Old French proverb

MONEY, POPULAR CULTURE TEACHES, cannot buy happiness. We have plenty of examples, and lots of data, to back that up. Consider that:

- An estimated one-third of lottery winners end up broke within five years, and a significant percentage of the rest report problems in their relations with families, friends, and co-workers.

- Rapper MC Hammer, developer Donald Trump, boxer Mike Tyson, and former Presidents Ulysses S. Grant and Thomas Jefferson are just a few examples of people who went broke after enjoying the kind of success that should have guaranteed financial independence.

...people who said money is the most important factor in their lives were the unhappiest.

- Numerous psychological studies find that money has no effect on a person's innate sense of well-being. If you were happy before you had money, you were happy after. If you were paranoid and suspicious before, you were more so after.

- Research by Kennon Sheldon, a psychologist at the University of Missouri at Columbia, found consistently that people who said money is the most important factor in their lives are the unhappiest.

Financial independence is not about your bank balance. It's about having your money under control, being clear about your financial goals, and achieving those goals in a methodical fashion. What's holding you back from a future free of money worries may be the faulty principles you've been fed that undermine your goal of living your life without assistance from others, which includes your employer.

To begin reframing your attitude about money, imagine a typical day in your life once you've achieved financial independence.

If you were financially independent...

What time would you wake up?
What would you do first? Second?
When and what would you eat?
What kind of car would you drive?
What kind of home would you live in?
What would be your main
   activity that day?
How would you spend the evening?
When would you go to bed?

Out of this kind of exercise you should be able to begin personalizing your financial plan. If self-direction, self-governance, and autonomy are important concepts for you, you need to figure out what that means for your personality, family situation, values, and goals. Before we talk about accumulating money, it's essential to know what you need it for.

RETIRING THE RETIREMENT CONCEPT

Everywhere you turn, the investment industry talks to you about retirement. It's a term that baby boomers are in the process of retiring from their vocabulary. Our values have changed since the days when Dad worked at the same company for thirty years and then he and Mom moved to Florida to await the grim reaper in tropical comfort. Today, the majority of Americans expect to work to age seventy, even if they don't have to, expect their lifestyles and expenses to remain about the same, and plan to finish out their lives either in their current homes, or within twenty-five miles.

You are financially independent when you work only because you want to, not because you must.

One of the more fascinating findings in recent polls on retirement attitudes is that most people place greatest emphasis on health, both mental and physical, and very little on financial independence. The ironies in this multiply themselves. If you don't take care of your financial independence you risk greater stress, which leads to poorer health at a time when you may be least able to afford the best care.

In my discussions with clients about creating wealth, financial independence is not the goal but the foundation for everything else. You are financially independent when you work only because you want to, not because you must.

Women statistically outlive men, and I observe that it has less to do with gender differences in health than differences in how we think about our lives. Women, whether they work or not, have fuller social lives that include children, friends, hobbies, and so on. They instinctively seem to know how to give their lives meaning when work is no longer the focus. Men live lives that are tightly focused on career. We men may dream of quitting work and having unlimited free time, but too often we have no plan, no idea what to do next.

Thurgood Marshall, the first African-American to serve on the U.S. Supreme Court, told a reporter that he could not imagine doing anything else but serving on the court. He said that if he quit, he would probably die of boredom. When he finally retired in 1991 at the age of 83, he said, "I'm getting old and coming apart." He died eighteen months later.

Retirement is not all it's advertised to be, and financial independence is more than owning your home free and clear.

Retirement is not all it's advertised to be, and financial independence is more than owning your home free and clear.

AUTONOMY FUNDS*

If you can switch from thinking about money as the key to owning your future, and start thinking about what it means to you to own your future, and then how you can achieve that financially, you'll be far more motivated and therefore successful in reaching your goals.

> *Autonomy funds are the assets you need to achieve your freedom from outside influence.*

Many people misunderstand how money works in their lives. Dan Sullivan, founder of The Strategic Coach®, who helps entrepreneurs struggling to balance life and work, observes that, "Poverty is not a scarcity of actual money, but a scarcity of vision."

Money should follow vision—not the other way around. When you bought your first car or your first house, these short-term financial goals began with a vision of what you wanted. You researched your options, compared prices, determined how hard you needed to work and for how long in order to accumulate the funds for a down payment.

For some reason people seem to have a problem applying this same process to setting life goals. If you apply it to all aspects of your life rather than one specific goal at one period of time, you've got the basic principal of "autonomy funds." Autonomy means freedom from outside influence. Autonomy funds are the assets you need to achieve your freedom from outside influence.

Colleges, universities, and similar nonprofit entities live and die by this principal. The goal of most fundraising activity is to create endowments that will guarantee the long term success of research, programs, or scholarships. Take this same fundraising concept and apply it to your personal life and you have a financial framework within which to plan your financial future.

The formula for success is simple:

(Goals & Vision) x Action = Money and Independence

SETTING UP YOUR AUTONOMY FUNDS

Most people approach financial planning by looking backward, which is like trying to drive by looking in the rearview mirror. It typically begins—and ends—with the hardest question for most families to answer: where does all the money

---

* The conceptual basis of The Autonomy Funds is inspired by, and draws information from, the discussion of Autonomy Funds in Goal Cultivator 7, a publication of The Strategic Coach, Inc. The Autonomy Funds is a trademark, copyright and integral concept of The Strategic Coach, Inc. All rights reserved. Used with written permission. For more information about The Strategic Coach® review their website at www.strategiccoach.com.

go? It's important to know where you are before you decide where you want to go, but so often people get stuck at that point. They know how much they need to live on today, and they think all they need to do is figure out how to keep that amount coming in.

At the end of this chapter you'll find a typical cash flow budget that many investment advisors ask clients to fill out to begin the financial planning process. It's two pages long, with dozens of categories, right down to your water and sewer bill–and it's the wrong approach. Financial planning is not about record-keeping and mathematics, but that's where it ends for most. I would put crunching numbers near the end of the process, not the beginning. It shouldn't be so intimidating and overwhelming. Besides, looking back serves to remind us of our mistakes—the money squandered foolishly, wealth invested badly, the opportunities overlooked. The planning process should begin with hope, not regret.

Financial planning is not about record-keeping and mathematics, but that's where it ends for most.

Another common mistake is that people tend to adapt their lifestyles to their income rather than making their income serve their lifestyle. The autonomy funds approach puts the setting of broad lifestyle goals at the front of your financial planning, forcing you to look forward, and simplifying the process.

Instead of the fifty or so categories of spending that a typical cash flow budget asks you to identify, our lives can be divided into twelve accounts that define your financial universe. We can group those twelve categories into three principal areas of our financial lives: protection, savings, and wealth.

...people tend to adapt their lifestyles to their income rather than making their income serve their lifestyle.

You may name these categories any way that appeals to you, and you can add categories to suit your particular lifestyle. The purpose of this exercise is to show you how to simplify the process and widen your financial horizons.

On the following pages you will find a graph that shows the relationship between these categories, and a chart showing what each category includes, followed by a blank form on which you can pencil in your information and see how it works. At the end you'll find an example that illustrates why my father could retire eight years before he thought he could.

Breaking It Down To Build It Up

YOUR FINANCIAL LIFE CAN BE DIVIDED INTO SOME BASIC CATEGORIES.

By thinking about which is more or less important, you can begin to weave together your individual life goals into a plan that helps you make financial choices that support it. Once you've pondered the breakdown below, use the blank version on the next page to write down the specifics of your own goals in each category. People who go through this process often report the results surprising and inspiring.

AUTONOMY FUNDS*

Fund	Purpose	Key Goals
Wealth	*Legacy*	*Growth*
Asset Support	Meet mortgage and similar obligations	Real estate growth
Unique Opportunity	Take advantage of special situations	Business investment returns
Taxes	Meet obligations	Minimize tax bite
Savings	*Life Style*	*Foundation*
System Support	Basic necessities	Maintenance
Gratitude	To show appreciation to people and institutions.	Charity
Walk Away	To retire with a feeling of financial independence	Peace of mind
Free Time	To maintain or improve quality of life and leisure.	Comfort, reward
Education	Meet tuition needs	Family support
Entertainment	Special events: weddings, parties, travel	Socialization
Protection	*Security*	*Reliability*
Big Picture	Long-range goals and planning	Reserves and insurance
Wellness	Longevity and disease prevention services	Productivity, lower medical expenses
Legacy	Grow and ensure inheritance	Guarantee bequests

What's YOUR Vision of the Future?

AUTONOMY FUNDS*

Fund	Purpose	Key Goals
Wealth	Legacy	Growth
Asset Support		
Unique Opportunity		
Taxes		
Savings	Life Style	Foundation
System Support		
Gratitude		
Walk Away		
Free Time		
Education		
Entertainment		
Protection	Security	Reliability
Big Picture		
Wellness		
Legacy		

* The conceptual basis of The Autonomy Funds is inspired by, and draws information from, the discussion of Autonomy Funds in Goal Cultivator 7, a publication of The Strategic Coach, Inc. The Autonomy Funds is a trademark, copyright and integral concept of The Strategic Coach, Inc. All rights reserved. Used with written permission. For more information about The Strategic Coach® review their website at www.strategiccoach.com.

A Typical Cash Flow Budget...

The Personal Budget

Worksheet

Name: _____

Period covered - From: _____ To: _____

Item	Historical	Current Budget	Current Actual	Difference
Food				
Home consumption	$_____	$_____	$_____	$_____
Outside the home	$_____	$_____	$_____	$_____
Total food:	$_____	$_____	$_____	$_____
Clothing				
Clothing and shoes	$_____	$_____	$_____	$_____
Cleaning, laundry	$_____	$_____	$_____	$_____
Jewelry, watches, etc.	$_____	$_____	$_____	$_____
Total clothing:	$_____	$_____	$_____	$_____
Housing				
Rent or mortgage	$_____	$_____	$_____	$_____
Real estate taxes	$_____	$_____	$_____	$_____
Insurance	$_____	$_____	$_____	$_____
Furniture and furnishings	$_____	$_____	$_____	$_____
Appliances	$_____	$_____	$_____	$_____
Cleaning, repairs and maint.	$_____	$_____	$_____	$_____
Electricity, gas and heating	$_____	$_____	$_____	$_____
Water and sewer	$_____	$_____	$_____	$_____
Telephone, cable	$_____	$_____	$_____	$_____
Other housing	$_____	$_____	$_____	$_____
Total housing:	$_____	$_____	$_____	$_____
Personal and Legal				
Personal care and toiletries	$_____	$_____	$_____	$_____
Child care	$_____	$_____	$_____	$_____
Legal and accounting	$_____	$_____	$_____	$_____
Life and disability insurance	$_____	$_____	$_____	$_____
Other personal and legal	$_____	$_____	$_____	$_____
Total personal and legal:	$_____	$_____	$_____	$_____
Medical				
Medicines	$_____	$_____	$_____	$_____
Doctors, dentists and hospitals	$_____	$_____	$_____	$_____
Health insurance	$_____	$_____	$_____	$_____
Other medical	$_____	$_____	$_____	$_____
Total medical:	$_____	$_____	$_____	$_____
Totals for this page:	$_____	$_____	$_____	$_____

...Is Often Too Complex

The Personal Budget

Worksheet

Name: _____

Period covered - From: _____ To: _____

Item	Historical	Current Budget	Current Actual	Difference
Transportation				
Auto payments	$_____	$_____	$_____	$_____
Repairs and maintenance	$_____	$_____	$_____	$_____
Insurance	$_____	$_____	$_____	$_____
Gas, oil and tires	$_____	$_____	$_____	$_____
Public transportation	$_____	$_____	$_____	$_____
Other transportation	$_____	$_____	$_____	$_____
Total transportation:	$_____	$_____	$_____	$_____
Miscellaneous				
Books, magazines and newspapers	$_____	$_____	$_____	$_____
Vacations	$_____	$_____	$_____	$_____
Entertainment and clubs	$_____	$_____	$_____	$_____
Charitable	$_____	$_____	$_____	$_____
Education	$_____	$_____	$_____	$_____
Other miscellaneous	$_____	$_____	$_____	$_____
Total miscellaneous:	$_____	$_____	$_____	$_____
Debt, savings and investment				
Credit and charge cards	$_____	$_____	$_____	$_____
Other installment loans	$_____	$_____	$_____	$_____
Education fund	$_____	$_____	$_____	$_____
Retirement	$_____	$_____	$_____	$_____
Other savings goals	$_____	$_____	$_____	$_____
Other	$_____	$_____	$_____	$_____
Total debt, savings and investment:	$_____	$_____	$_____	$_____
Totals for this page:	$_____	$_____	$_____	$_____
Totals from previous page:	$_____	$_____	$_____	$_____
Grand totals:	$_____	$_____	$_____	$_____

AUTONOMY FUNDS AND GOAL SETTING

Once you have established general categories for your autonomy funds, you can then group your expenditures into single figures and create targeted funds to endow each account, just as colleges do.

EXAMPLE:

Assume the only asset in your Asset Support Fund is your home on which you have a mortgage. Suppose you want to retire in fifteen years and, based on your current payments, you will still owe $100,000 on a 6 percent mortgage. You're in the 33 percent tax bracket but you haven't been contributing as much as you could to your 401(k), and want to retire mortgage free.

Assuming a loan balance at retirement of $100,000 at 6 percent:

Option 1: After Tax Pay-Down

If you contribute an extra $840 per month in after-tax dollars for 15 years, you'll pay the mortgage off. But that's actually costing you $1,250 per month in cash flow—you have to earn $1,250 to net $840 after taxes.

Option 2: Pre-Tax Investment

Maintain your regular mortgage payment but contribute $1,250 per month (pre-tax) over the next 15 years to a fixed account with your employer's 401(k) yielding a modest 5 percent. At the end of 15 years, you will have accumulated $335,000. But you only need $100,000 to pay off your mortgage. You own your house and you've got $235,000 left over to support other goals.

Economics is all about financial incentives. The trick is to create financial incentives in your life and use them as the basis of your financial planning.

6 Your Financial Blueprint

> *Strategic planning is worthless—*
> *unless there is first a strategic vision.*
> —John Naisbitt, author of Megatrends

THE WORLD IS DROWNING in financial planners. From your local banker, to your insurance agent, your stockbroker, accountants, lawyers—they all call themselves financial planners.

The financial planning industry is relatively young, and it evolved along with the other trends I discussed earlier—the development of investment products and the need to have salesmen to peddle them. The innovators in this new industry decided that if they could create a professional air about financial planning, it would be easier to sell their products. Financial planners would automatically get the kind of respect afforded doctors and lawyers.

But unlike doctors and lawyers, when the financial planning industry began to pick up steam, clients resisted paying financial professionals for their expertise. Why, some argued, should I pay for advice when I can just buy a no- or low-load mutual fund and go along for the ride?

Would you rather have surgery performed by a doctor paid by you, or one who is free but earns a commission from the drug company, the company that made the medical equipment, and the hospital to whose operating room he steers his patients?

As a result, companies wanting to sell their investment products based their compensation of financial planners on commissions. They offered higher commissions on products that earned the company the biggest profit. None of this has anything to do with the client's best interests, and the system is one of the most common and unseen conflicts of interest in the investment industry.

Investments are often purchased not as part of a strategy, but when a problem has developed. A successful financial plan integrates all the different areas of your life.

Would you rather have surgery performed by a doctor paid by you, or one who is free but earns a commission from the drug company, the company that made the medical equipment, and the hospital to whose operating room he steers his patients? Which doctor is looking out for you? The same holds true for many financial planners to whom you are a customer who can buy their products, not a person who needs help reaching his or her life goals.

Picture your current financial state as a building housing your wealth—a home that shelters your future. Your financial home, just like the home you live in, is divided into different areas designed to meet the different aspects of your life.

All financial products are intended to serve one of three needs in a financial life: assets for protection; financial products and services for savings; or investments aimed at building wealth. Each "room" in your financial shelter offers a myriad of solutions to address the need. These solutions are called investment products, whether it's a mutual fund, an insurance policy, or an equity investment.

Too many people get stuck trying to analyze the products being sold by the salespeople—is this a good investment or not—while ignoring the big picture. The investment industry wants customers to purchase an investment product to fit in each category. The investment might solve a specific issue and perform as required, but the rest of the plan may fall apart if all these products are not integrated.

It often shocks clients when I show them that in one "room" they have sold a poorly performing investment, only to buy it back without realizing it is part of an investment product purchased for another purpose. I have had clients come to me with three dozen different investment accounts and no clue how they interact with each other.

The investment industry hype is hard to resist. Many consumers unwittingly sacrifice security in one area to protect themselves in another. Investments are often purchased not as part of a strategy, but when a problem has developed. A successful financial plan integrates all the different areas of your life.

ASSET MANAGEMENT STAGES

Institutionally Managed

Strategic Asset Allocation

Self-Managed Portfolio

Tactical Asset Allocation

WEALTH ACCUMULATION STAGE

Elements include:
Art & Antiques; Real Estate; Business
Equity; Income Stocks & Funds;
Index/Exchange Traded Funds;
Growth Stocks & Funds; Government,
Municipal, and Corporate Bonds

FINANCIAL SECURITY STAGE

Elements include:
After-Tax Tax-Deferred or Tax-Free
Savings, and Pre-Tax Tax-Deferred
Savings; U.S. Bonds/Treasury Bills/
Notes; CDs, Money Market, Savings,
Credit Union, & Checking Accounts

FINANCIAL FOUNDATION

Elements include:
Wills & Trusts; Titling of Assets; Life
Insurance; Disability, Health, & Long-
Term Care Insurance; Home, Auto,
Property & Liability Insurance.

THE FEAR-FACTOR FINANCIAL PLAN

What are you most concerned about right now in your financial planning? You might have children who will be going to college, or maybe your principal issue is making sure you have a secure retirement, or that your expenses will be covered if you were faced with a serious disability. Typical financial planning would address each of these three areas separately, and that would be a mistake.

If it's college tuition you're concerned about, most financial planners will begin by running a computer program that produces a thirty-five page report showing that you'll need about a quarter-million dollars per child. Once you've picked yourself up off the floor, the planner will likely try to sell you a 529 College Savings Fund, a state-sponsored program that lets you put away money that earns tax-free income so long as the money is used for educational purposes.

The computer spits out a thirty-five page report that will likely scare the hell out of you. It may say that you'll have to work longer, save more, and increase the risk in your portfolio in hopes of achieving a better return.

Next, the planner will turn his attention to your retirement. Once again, his computer is filled with all kinds of information about your current retirement savings and your projected benefit from your employer. The computer spits out another thirty-five page report that will likely scare the hell out of you. It may say that you'll have to work longer, save more, and increase the risk in your portfolio in hopes of achieving a better return.

These depressing projections will be based on average return assumptions that, as you'll read later, are faulty and misleading. But the point is to get you to buy a

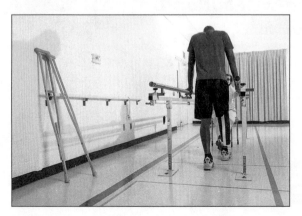

retirement plan. Now you have a college savings plan and a retirement plan.

Finally, the planner assesses your financial vulnerability if you should become disabled. Your ability to work is your most valuable asset. If you haven't been terrified by the outlook produced by the first two analyses he's done, it then becomes the job of the planner to convince you that, immediately upon departing his office, you will be run over by a car. That persuades you to buy another investment product—the disability plan that insures 60 percent of your salary.

You leave the office, look both ways before crossing the street, and go on with your life thinking you've covered all the bases. Not so fast.

You'll be able to pay your bills while you're lying in the hospital, but now you don't have enough money to continue funding your 529 College Savings Plan. You are no longer earning credits or a contribution for retirement. The whole financial plan falls apart.

GETTING OUT OF THE PRODUCT BOX

Each category of an integrated financial plan—Protection, Savings, Wealth—should include investments that will serve more than one purpose.

For financial protection, you invest and use services to protect your assets—your car, your home, and so on. You purchase liability insurance in case you're sued, so you won't lose what you've already accumulated. If you move up a level, you can invest to protect both your assets and your income so that if you are disabled you'll have the income to pay your bills, and medical insurance to cover hospital costs.

One level higher, you can buy financial products and services to protect your assets and income beyond your lifetime, to protect your heirs. You create such protection through wills or trusts, and how you create or title your assets. It's not uncommon for lawyers to write wills and trusts that fail to take into account how your assets are titled, or other arrangements, and it ends up costing your beneficiaries a fortune in legal and accounting bills to straighten it all out.

Life insurance, the kind being heavily marketed today by the investment industry as a great investment and a way to protect your assets after death, is a terrible idea and a bad investment. The right kind of life insurance—boring, old-fashioned, dividend-paying, whole life contracts—can meet more needs than any other single investment. This is life insurance where you are both customer and owner. You will find more detail about life insurance in Part VII, "Making Sense of Insurance." It is, in many ways, the most important concept you'll need to understand in putting together a superior financial plan.

> *Life insurance, the kind heavily marketed today by the investment industry as a great investment and a way to protect your assets after death, is a terrible idea and a bad investment.*

SAVINGS: THE FINANCIAL SECURITY STAGE

At the least, you need to save some cash for emergencies and other uses that require immediate access. If you move up to the second level, you trade some liquidity for a higher return, but your money is still available for emergencies. One level higher, and you can have savings that will earn an even higher rate of return thanks to tax benefits.

The pre-tax, tax-deferred category of savings provides income for the future. While this area is the easiest place to save in a typical financial plan, there are drawbacks. When you withdraw funds, they are taxed at ordinary\income tax rates and Uncle Sam controls the rate at which you can spend it.

WEALTH: THE FINANCIAL ACCUMULATION STAGE

Opportunities for the greatest returns usually require large lump sums of money. For an investment opportunity to reach its potential, you will most often need some type of deposit or capital investment, especially if the opportunity falls into an ownership category. It's important to remember that the older you get, the more important it is to have after-tax assets.

The first level of after-tax assets are bonds, although they historically can't keep up with inflation because the return is usually taxed as ordinary income. Also, bonds don't meet the ownership threshold that we're trying to maintain. As a bond buyer, you are a lender and in that equation it is the borrower who has control.

Stocks are an after-tax asset that put you in the position of owner. Stocks historically have a higher return, with more risk and volatility. But, stock owner-

The highest level for the accumulation of true wealth is through genuine ownership of tangible assets such as real estate.

ship comes with the benefit of lower capital gains tax rates and the ability to offset gains with losses.

The highest level for the accumulation of true wealth is through genuine ownership of tangible assets such as real estate. As an investor at this level, you pay no tax on the increase in the value of the property until you sell it, and even then, you benefit from favorable treatment under current tax laws. This is wealth you can leverage by using someone else's money to fund your investment, like being on the borrower side of a bond transaction. As the borrower, you control the lending relationship, you benefit from the funds, and you accumulate wealth faster.

INTEGRATION: THE ASSET MANAGEMENT STAGE

...determining how your money should be managed and by whom is one of the most important decisions you'll make, and that you should expect there to be a cost for good advice. Free never is.

In your life you have many potential experts to help you plan your financial life: accountants, lawyers, stockbrokers, money managers, insurance agents, human resource managers. Each may be ethical and competent but often their knowledge is specific to their professions. Without a coordinated plan, you have a high risk of failing.

It's common in my business to have new clients who have accumulated significant wealth and think that they can manage it using advice from a television business program or a self-help financial book. Understanding the tax code and making simple changes in investments–what you own and where you put it–often can yield an additional 15 to 20 percent greater wealth over a lifetime of invest-ment. By developing an integrated financial plan, you can reduce your investment risk while boosting the rewards.

By now you should have signed on to the idea that determining how your money should be managed and by whom is one of the most important decisions you'll make, and that you should expect there to be a cost for good advice. Free never is. Your choices ought to be made looking forward rather than out of fear; in a holistic fashion, not on the basis of a sales-pitch or a 35-page computer printout; and it should be made to suit your specific situation, not a formula you read about in a magazine.

7 Being Your Own Bank

> *Waste neither time nor money,*
> *but make the best use of both.*
> *–Benjamin Franklin*

A VAST AMOUNT OF WEALTH is squandered when people use everyday banking techniques. What if you created your own bank?

Every single thing we do in life has a cost. If we could create a method to recoup these accumulated costs, think of the millions of dollars we could recover!

Wealth Creation Truth #3: Everything in life has a cost and requires payments. To get by in life, we must either make payments into savings accounts OR make payments from savings into capital expenditures.

Consider an everyday purchase—buying a car for, say, $20,000. How should you pay for this purchase, with cash from savings or an auto loan? Let's assume your savings account earns 6 percent, and the auto loan will cost 7.5 percent. Most people assume that cash is cheaper because the rate is lower. But if one were to finance the car purchase using someone else's money, it would have saved them about $2,000 because $20,000 earning a steady and compounding 6 percent ends up more–$26,000 after five years–than paying 7.5 percent on a declining-balance car loan: about $24,000.

In order to accumulate enough savings to pay for the car, you had to make payments into an account. When you apply those payments (or savings) toward the purchase of a car, they should be re-categorized as "car payments made in advance."

Wealth Creation Truth #3: Everything in life has a cost and requires payments. To get by in life, we must either make payments into savings accounts OR make payments from savings into capital expenditures.

YOUR OWN PERSONAL BANK

Instead of directing your payments into a financial institution, you could control the account into which you regularly make deposits.

Let's look at three payment options we can use to pay for the purchase of large, tangible assets: cash, financing through some third party (bank), or through the use of what we call an **Integrated Independence Account**®. All three options are based in some method on financing.

All financing includes one or more monthly payments at some cost, whether that cost is paid as interest to a lender, or as interest earnings lost when we redirect funds from investment to consumption. Financing is a process and the choices made determine who profits from the transaction. If you have the choice between letting the bank profit, or keeping that profit, the choice is clear.

The goal of the Integrated Independence Account, or being your own bank, is to recover interest that one normally pays to a banking institution. The underlying principle is that any time the payment of interest to others can be redirected to another vehicle you own and control that offers the same market rate of interest (subject to minimal taxation), individual wealth will have grown.

The average American spends roughly a third of every dollar on interest expense and roughly a third of every dollar in taxes.

The average American spends roughly a third of every dollar on interest expense and roughly a third of every dollar in taxes. If we can recapture any portion of our interest and tax expenses, we should be able to create sizable wealth for ourselves and families, and achieve returns relatively greater than the market.

THE CASH OPTION AUTOMOBILE PURCHASE

If we have the cash on hand to purchase a car outright, it means we have previously made payments into a bank account over a period of years to accumulate the pool of funds necessary. The funds could have been contributed to a cash type savings account over a five-year period, with a steady, low-risk rate of return: 2 percent for this illustration. Assume that taxes on those interest earnings will be about a third, so the net return will be 1.34 percent.

To purchase a $30,000 car every five years for the next 30 years, payments could be made in advance into the bank account at $600 a month. The balance in the account at the end of each five-year period, when you're ready to buy a new car, will be about $37,000, of which $30,000 will go toward buying the car, and the rest can be transferred to a long term fund, earning a hypothetical 4 percent return after taxes.

But there are even better options.

LIFE INSURANCE AS A BANK

Suppose, instead of saving money in a bank, you put that same money into a participating whole life insurance contract, which is a financial vehicle that you own. Your contract accumulates cash value against which you can borrow and, unlike a bank, you can decide how or whether to pay the money back in. Most importantly, you'll incur no fees and receive guaranteed credit approval. You will learn more about how insurance works in Part V, but here is a simple illustration.

Your options are:

1. Don't pay back the money. You will effectively be treating your insurance contract the same as a bank account. If you borrow $20,000 from a life insurance policy that pays you a 6 percent dividend, you will lose the $1,200 per year you would have earned on the money you borrowed from your cash value. So that's your cost, $1,200 per year, and a reduction in your cash value.

2. Pay back interest only. If you pay $1,200 each year into your life insurance contract, it will be deposited back into your cash value, so you've reduced your cash value but not lost any income.

3. Maintain the same payments of principal and interest. You can replenish the $20,000 by making payments into your life insurance contract of $400 a month for five years, to replace the $20,000 you borrowed. At the end of 5 years, you will have paid back into your insurance policy the full $24,045. Thus you will have borrowed $20,000 from yourself to buy a car, then paid yourself back with interest.

In this way, you can recapture the cost of anything you do, whether it's a car every five years or something much more costly like college tuition.

PAYMENTS TO YOUR BANK INSTEAD OF THEIRS

Throughout all these discussions, our goal is to explode the myths of traditional financial practices. Payments need to be made constantly over one's lifetime, either in the form of savings or expenditures. How we apply those payments can determine success or failure.

Banks encourage us to save and park our money so that they can move our dollars through various financial transactions in order to create their wealth. Companies encourage us to buy their shares so that they can take our parked dollars and move them to acquire other companies in order to create wealth.

This process has created tremendous wealth for businesses. If companies and governments can utilize these strategies, why shouldn't individuals be able to create the wealth and security for our families in the same way? When you learn the techniques of wealth creation by the use of certain financial products, you can enjoy a better life without having to assume unnecessary risk.

When you learn the techniques of wealth creation by the use of certain financial products, you can enjoy a better life without having to assume unnecessary risk.

PART III

Stocks and Stats:
Myth vs. Reality

8 Myths of Averages, Benchmarks, and Indexing

ON WALL STREET, as in politics, things often aren't as they appear.

Financial gurus have been telling us for decades that, statistically, the stock market provides the greatest consistent profit, with long-term annual returns averaging 10.7 percent. On that basis alone, trillions of dollars have been invested in the stock markets.

The problem: it's a myth, a statistical untruth (as opposed to an outright lie). The 10.7 percent figure is based on a long period of time, 1926 through 2001, and it is arrived at by compounding. That means this statistic is based on the preposterous assumption that you invested your money in a stock market index and left it there for seventy-six years.

No one invests for seventy-six years, so this information has little value to anyone inhabiting the real world. Furthermore, the notion that the market reliably returns 10.7 percent a year is simply false.

How The Numbers Lie:

The Myth of Stock Market Returns

- The Dow Jones Industrial Average flirted with a high of 1000 for the first time in 1966. It took sixteen years, until 1982, to break through and stay above that level. Average annual return after inflation: -4 percent.

- If you took the plunge in 1990 with a ten-year horizon, you struck it rich. The Dow returned an annual average of 18.2 percent.

- Out of the 57 possible 20-year slices of the past 76 years, 22 fell below 10.7 percent. Over the entire 57 slices, returns ranged between 3.1 and 17.9 percent. Assuming you started with $100,000, you could have ended up with as little as $185,000 and as much as $2.7 million.

In the real world, each of us enters the market at different times and at different points in the cycle. No one can guarantee that any particular time period is going to meet or exceed the average. If predictability is more important to you than the risk inherent in betting on a good market, you should be cautious about how much of your portfolio you keep in equities. Cautious investors will sleep better owning bonds and saving more of their earnings. Stocks aren't the only way to create wealth.

THE DEFLATING EFFECT OF INFLATION

Investing is similar to bailing out a leaky boat. You have to bail faster than the water comes in or you'll eventually sink.

Your money loses buying power every minute of every day. Slowly and inexorably, the cost of living goes up and your buying power leaks away. In order to just keep even, your investment profits must at least equal the constantly rising tide of inflation. To create wealth, your returns must exceed inflation, the more the better.

While inflation can boost the return on certain financial assets such as CDs, high inflation is ruinous, as it was when it ran amok in the late 1970s and early 1980s, reaching a high of 13 percent in 1979. Bankruptcies in 1982 reached an all-time record.

To create wealth, your returns must exceed inflation, the more the better.

As important as it is to know how your investments are faring relative to inflation, the investment industry would rather not discuss it. Brokers and other investment sales people would rather talk about the fabulous returns in the stock market between 1982–the rock bottom–and 2000–the absolute top. From bottom to top, the Dow rose from just under 800 to 12,000, a spectacular annualized return of 16 percent. What is rarely mentioned is that inflation during that same period averaged more than 3 percent a year.

It serves Wall Street's interests to overstate the actual purchasing-power gains won by past investors, and does a great disservice to today's investors. Nominal numbers over long time spans are meaningless. True gains are only relevant when measured against their purchasing power.

Real Versus Reported Returns

Inflation retards the gains investors earn during bull markets. In the 1950s and 1960s, reported gains were well over 500 percent. But after inflation—in Wall Street parlance, "real terms"—investors lost more than a third of the profit to inflation.

All investors, and particularly stock investors, need to keep this concept in mind at all times. The math of inflation is pernicious when stock prices are flat or declining because it deepens the real losses borne by investors, and makes it much harder to catch up. We most recently saw this in the markets after the 1990s bubble, starting in 2000. Actual losses were worse than reported losses when you add in the effect of inflation, which works the same as returns, except instead of compounding profits it compounds the misery year by year.

How Inflation Compounds Losses

If you have $100,000 and your portfolio loses 7 percent in one year and inflation is steady at 3 percent, you end the year with $90,000. In order to get back to where you were and not lose any purchasing power, your return for the following year has to be at least 14.4 percent. Anything less than that and you're sinking faster than you can bail.

Perhaps the most extreme example of the myth of averages can be found in the performance of the Standard & Poor's 500 average between November 1968 and March 1995, after adjusted for inflation. Investors buying at the 1960s top would have waited more than a quarter of a century before they earned even one additional percent of purchasing power!

If an average investor starts investing at age twenty-five and retires at sixty-five, he or she has four decades in which to accumulate wealth–to grow their nest egg. Although stocks have produced average annual double-digit profits over the very long haul, the market sometimes falls and stays down for extended periods. In the real world we face economic emergencies that require ready cash. If you have the bad luck to need cash during a bad market patch and need to sell instead of holding on for better days, you can blow a huge hole in your wealth plans.

COMPOUNDING THE CONFUSION

Market investments such as stocks and bonds are evaluated on the basis of compound return. But the basis of much of today's financial planning intended to calculate how much you'll need to retire, or meet tuition payments, or reach your other goals is based on compound interest–what the bank or other guaranteed accounts pay.

This is a mistaken formula, as I've demonstrated earlier. Compound interest is typically fixed and reliable. Each year you earn interest on your principal and interest on the interest you've earned in previous years. It's not as exciting as stocks, without a chance to participate in bull markets like the one we lived through in the 1990s. But just in case you don't get into and out of the market at the right points in the cycle, a lower rate of return that has consistent compounding can produce a bigger profit.

...you can massage the numbers many different ways to produce many different and conflicting pictures of the same thing.

Average rates of return are just as irrelevant in financial planning as they are in predicting the stock market. So is the related term, Total Return. Yet these are the two most significant measurement tools used in the investment industry to promote mutual funds. Nearly all mutual fund marketing materials brag about rates of return, with fancy graphics and upward-trending charts. They show the returns for one year, five years, ten years, and sometimes even longer.

But these numbers should not be used in financial planning because they don't reflect the real world in which investors enter and leave the market at different times. As we've seen, you can massage the numbers many different ways to produce many different and conflicting pictures of the same thing.

When I ask clients what they think the average annualized return is on a mutual fund that has grown 200 percent in ten years, almost every one immediately divides the total return by ten to come up with 20 percent. Their jaws drop when I prove to them that the mathematical answer is 11.61 percent.

This erroneous thinking has been around for years, and has been perpetuated by the press. When Individual Retirement Accounts first became available, there were many articles projecting that an investor could end up with a million dollars over thirty-six years just by investing $2,000. But the assumption was a return of 12 percent. As this is written, money market rates are about 5 percent. What a disaster for the poor soul who believed in that tooth fairy! Inaccurate math can wreak havoc on a financial plan and rob you of your financial independence.

Inaccurate math can wreak havoc on a financial plan and rob you of your financial independence.

The following chart depicts the difference between average returns and actual returns of the four major markets over a six-year period. Be careful not to let the average rate of return calculation creep into your financial planning or conversations with any financial advisors.

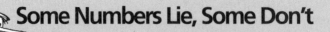

Some Numbers Lie, Some Don't

NUMBERS THAT LIE WHILE LOOKING GOOD:

Market Averages 1999–2004

Total return (six years) / annual average return

S&P 500: Total 17.52% / Average 2.92%

Int'l Stock Index: Total 34.25% / Average 5.71%

NASDAQ: Total 55.88% / Average 9.31%

Bond Index: Total 37.94% / Average 6.32%

Based on these figures, if you put $100,000 into each of these four markets at the start of 1999, by the end of 2004 your NASDAQ investment would have been the winner by far, finishing at $170,000. But that's not the way it works.

NUMBERS THAT CANNOT TELL A LIE:

Total REAL Market Returns 1999-2004 (six years)

S&P 500: 1.25% (NOT 17.52% as above)

Int'l Stock Index: 3.07% (NOT 34.25% as above)

NASDAQ: 0.50% (NOT 55.88% as above)

Bond Index: 6.24% (NOT 37.94% as above)

Based on these REAL figures, if you put $100,000 into each of these four markets at the start of 1999, by the end of 2004 every one would have lost your money, NOT including taxes, fees, inflation and so on. Your NASDAQ investment would have done the worst, losing you $68,000! Even your bond investment would have lost money, but only $700.

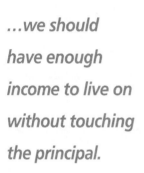

...we should have enough income to live on without touching the principal.

THE GREATEST RETIREMENT MISTAKE

The investment industry preaches that if we invest in the market and the market is true to its historical average return of roughly 10 percent, we should have enough income to live on without touching the principal. But as we've shown, average annual return is in somebody's imagination. Back here on Planet Earth, you'll realize much lower actual returns and have to spend your principal.

The following chart shows what we mean for someone who has a nest egg of $3 million and plans on that nice, steady 10 percent ($300,000 per year) he or she was told the stock market returns **on average** every year. Our confused investor has been led to believe that, after twenty years, he will have lived a comfy, worry-free retirement and still have a $3 million nest egg left over in case life turns out to be longer than planned, or to leave to the kids.

Nothing could be further from the reality.

Flawed Assumptions:
How to lose your shirt making money

Over 20 years, the stock market returns **on average** 10% a year. BUT **actual return** in the following example is only 7.8%. If you started with $3 million, expecting to live on $300,000 in stock market profits each year for 20 years, here's how you might have ended up. The result would be even worse if you added in the eroding effect of inflation, taxes, and fees.

Year	Market Return	Account Value	Account + Return	Payment to Ourselves	New Account Value
1	6%	$3,000,000.00	$3,180,000.00	$300,000.00	$2,880,000.00
2	14%	$2,880,000.00	$3,283,200.00	$300,000.00	$2,983,200.00
3	-5%	$2,983,200.00	$3,834,040.00	$300,000.00	$2,534,040.00
4	12%	$2,534,040.00	$3,838,124.80	$300,000.00	$2,538,124.80
5	11%	$2,538,124.80	$2,817,318.53	$300,000.00	$2,517,318.53
6	9%	$2,517,318.53	$2,743,877.20	$300,000.00	$2,443,877.20
7	14%	$2,443,877.20	$2,786,020.00	$300,000.00	$2,486,020.00
8	2%	$2,486,020.00	$2,535,740.40	$300,000.00	$2,235,740.40
9	-19%	$2,235,740.40	$1,810,949.73	$300,000.00	$1,510,949.73
10	15%	$1,510,949.73	$1,737,592.19	$300,000.00	$1,437,592.19
11	14%	$1,437,592.19	$1,638,855.09	$300,000.00	$1,338,855.09
12	7%	$1,338,855.09	$1,432,574.95	$300,000.00	$1,132,574.95
13	24%	$1,132,574.95	$1,404,392.94	$300,000.00	$1,104,392.94
14	18%	$1,104,392.94	$1,303,183.66	$300,000.00	$1,003,183.66
15	30%	$1,003,183.66	$1,304,138.76	$300,000.00	$1,004,138.76
16	15%	$1,004,138.76	$1,154,759.58	$300,000.00	$854,759.58
17	-5%	$854,759.58	$812,021.60	$300,000.00	$512,021.60
18	-6%	$512,021.60	$481,300.30	$300,000.00	$181,300.30
19	34%	$181,300.30	$242,942.40	$300,000.00	$57,057.60
20	10%	$57,057.60	$62,763.35	$300,000.00	**-$0-**
AVG.	**10%**	**ACTUAL 7.8%**		**RESULT: WEALTH LOST**	

For illustrative purposes only. Not indicative of individual results.
Assumes reinvestment of dividends and no effects of fees, taxes,
or erosion of buying power caused by inflation.

After twenty years, your $3 million nest egg is gone and you're left with Social Security. In all likelihood, the disaster would come sooner because of taxes and inflation.

Averages can work if compounding exists, time is on your side, and emotions are eliminated from the equation, which can only happen if an investor is not banking on a certain amount of income from market investments and can weather the ups and downs of the market. When you understand how averages work, you'll have a better basis for evaluating the best products or markets in which to invest.

When you understand how averages work, you'll have a better basis for evaluating the best products or markets in which to invest.

THE MYTH OF INDEX INVESTING

Mutual funds that invest solely in the stocks of a particular index, especially the S&P 500, became wildly popular in the 1990s as the stock markets kept rising. The Vanguard Index 500 Fund grew to become one of the largest in the entire industry on the strength of the popular idea that by exactly imitating the S&P 500 Index, you would out-perform most active money managers who toil away crunching numbers and picking stocks. This is an extraordinary claim: could it be that up to 95 percent of mutual fund mangers are so incompetent, or that their expenses are so high, that they can't even keep up with the average?

The answer is no. The reason that the S&P 500 Index mutual fund seems to outperform the active mutual fund manager is because that's comparing apples to oranges.

The S&P 500 Index is not truly representative because it is calculated on the total value of each company's underlying stock. That means General Electric (GE), which has billions of shares outstanding, will have a much greater impact on the performance

If you had invested in 1999 in the S&P 500 index thinking it was a safe, conservative way of being in the stock market, you could not have been more wrong. You were, in effect, investing in a technology fund that happened to have a bunch of other stocks in it as well.

of the S&P 500 Index than smaller companies like Genuine Parts (GPC). At this writing, GE's total value (total shares outstanding times stock price) is about 50 times greater than Genuine Parts. That means that if both companies' stocks rose by 10 percent, GE's increase will have 50 times as much of an impact on the S&P 500 Index than GPC's. This may be a good way to judge changes in the size of the overall U.S. economy, but it's a terrible way to invest.

How badly this can mislead is illustrated by what happened to the index in the 1990s. Because technology was the hottest sector of the stock market, technology stocks that were part of the S&P 500 rose much more. Their total value–their capitalization (number of shares outstanding times price per share)–reached a high of about 40 percent of the total S&P 500 value. If you had invested in 1999 in the S&P 500 index thinking it was a safe, conservative way of being in the stock market, you could not have been more wrong. You were, in effect, investing in a technology fund that happened to have a bunch of other stocks in it as well.

In 1999, the last full year of the big bull run, the top 50 stocks in the S&P 500 represented **more** than 100 percent of the gain in the total index for that year of 28.6 percent. This means that the remaining 450 stocks had little impact on the performance of the index. It also means that in 2000, after the market began to tank, those same stellar performers of 1999 became lead weights that had an exaggerated effect in dragging the market down. That means greater volatility, greater anxiety, greater risk, all of which we want to minimize.

An actively managed (stock picking) mutual fund manager invests based on what he or she thinks about the future performance of the companies, not on their size. If the fund had $100 million to invest, the manager might pick 50 or 60 great companies to invest in. But since he or she might not know which company or product concept is better than another, he might make an equally-weighted investment in each. He certainly wouldn't invest 50 times more in one company than another. It'd be putting too many eggs in one basket.

Even when the market is not obsessed with technology stocks, this flaw in the S&P 500 can be exaggerated by more prosaic companies. Supposedly "recession-proof" stocks like Coca Cola have, from time to time, plunged. Coke at one time lost 70 percent of its value; General Electric lost 60 percent; General Motors fell 66 percent; and Walt Disney at one point fell 85 percent. Each of these very large companies dragged the index down considerably.

You will see great returns when large companies do well, but you will get soundly trounced when things go wrong, as they inevitably do.

You will see great returns when large companies do well, but you will get soundly trounced when things go wrong, as they inevitably do.

WHY INDICES ARE BAD BENCHMARKS

As ludicrous as index investing may seem, it's equally ludicrous to evaluate the performance of your stock portfolio using the S&P 500 as a benchmark. Yet it is the industry standard and so many decisions are made based on this faulty concept. We compare the returns of our portfolio to the S&P, we rate the performance of mutual funds by ranking how well the fund manager outperformed or underperformed the index, and we measure the risk of a mutual fund or a manager relative to the S&P 500 Index.

The public appetite for indexing and the constant pressure on money managers to beat the index has created a self-reinforcing trend. Although there are 500 stocks in the index, the stocks at the top–Coca-Cola, Philip Morris, Microsoft, for example–are weighted several hundred times stocks at the bottom. The largest 10 or so companies have at times accounted for as much as half the aggregate value of the entire index.

So, when buying an S&P index fund, you're buying into the argument that Coca-Cola is really worth 200 times as much as the machine tool manufacturer, Giddings & Lewis. But what if Coke at that point is overvalued and Giddings & Lewis is undervalued? Tough luck.

...you are automatically becoming what is known as a momentum investor–the higher an S&P stock goes, the more of your index fund money will be invested in it. Adding highfliers and selling laggards means you're buying high, and selling low, the biggest single mistake any investor makes.

Thus you are automatically becoming what is known as a momentum investor–the higher an S&P stock goes, the more of your index fund money will be invested in it. Adding highfliers and selling laggards means you're buying high, and selling low, the biggest single mistake any investor makes.

In 2005, the top 10 percent of the index–the 50 largest companies–gained 23.4 percent, roughly 7 percent more than the average return of the remaining 450 stocks. The more the top companies outperform, the more money pours into them, and the more they outperform–as long as money keeps pouring into them.

This means that when a big company's stock is cheap and therefore a good value, an index fund buyer owns less of it. When it gets expensive, you own lots. This makes no sense, yet it is what you get when you invest in an index fund.

Since 1958, the year after the S&P 500 was created, an equally-weighted 500 index (based on the price of one share of every stock) would have outperformed the actual market-capitalization-weighted version (the total value of each company in the index) 60 percent of the time. In other words, most of the time the S&P 500 index presents a distorted view of investor sentiment and performance.

To make matters worse, investors who buy and hold index funds can never adjust their investments without selling out altogether. You can't take profits on an individual stock in an index fund. And everyone knows that an investing strategy or hot stock that works one year is at risk of unraveling the next.

One additional problem with the index is that companies are sometimes replaced in the index for what S&P calls "lack of representation." In other words, the S&P index committee believes that these companies no longer represent leading stocks in leading American industries. This allows arbitrariness to creep into the selection process. For instance, the S&P 500 has at times been underweighted in financial companies and overweighted in consumer nondurables.

The number of companies dropped for lack of representation has escalated in recent years. When you look at which stocks were dropped or added, you see some interesting patterns. There's nothing sinister about this. After all, the S&P 500 is a large-capitalization index, and it's only fitting that companies with diminished market value be exorcised. But adding highfliers and deleting the lowly means an investor in the S&P 500 is by default buying high and selling low.

Index funds are a dangerous placebo, giving many the illusion that the stock market is a much safer place than it really is. It's also produced wrong-headed thinking about the S&P's usefulness as a performance measurement tool. The S&P 500 average myth ignores a fundamental principal of investing: the risk of the investment as measured by volatility. By focusing solely on the investment's return, the glass can appear half full when it's really almost empty.

Index funds are a dangerous placebo, giving many the illusion that the stock market is a much safer place than it really is.

9 Risk, Emotion, and Lost Opportunity Cost

> *It is a curious fact that capital is generally most fearful when prices...are low and safe, and boldest at the heights when there is danger.*
> —Legendary investor Bernard M. Baruch

FROM THE GREAT DEPRESSION to the bursting of the 1990s tech bubble, economic disasters are embedded in our cultural subconcious and, like a recurring nightmare, inform how we think about financial risk. If that wasn't enough, we humans are programmed to make terrible choices when it comes to money and investments. There have been many studies, and there is plenty of data, that show beyond doubt that we are for some reason emotionally programmed to buy high and sell low.

A study entitled "Dumb Money," conducted by professors at Yale and University of Chicago, found that between 1983 and 2003, the hottest mutual

funds–those experiencing the greatest inflows of money–performed much worse than mutual funds that investors were dumping.

Over-simplified versions of history encourage us to assume that the Great Depression was caused by the stock market Crash of 1929. Between 1930 and 1933, stock prices did fall by about 80 percent. But what is often unmentioned is that, so long as one held their shares and the company stayed solvent, they still owned a chunk of it. They were still owners of something tangible.

When some 10,000 banks went broke, their depositors ended up with nothing, because they were lenders, not owners. They had "lent" their money to the bank in the form of deposits, and the banks lost it.

Out of the Depression was born the flawed but very popular notion that one of the surest signs of financial security was owing nothing to anyone, including owning your home free and clear. Thanks to the many banking and other reforms enacted during Franklin Roosevelt's New Deal years, insuring certain bank deposits for example, we got the idea that the safest place to put your money is in a savings account earning interest.

An entire generation came out of the Depression scarred by the experience, determined never to be caught in a similar situation again. Risk became associated with losing money, even though not everyone lost money.

Today, it can be a costly mistake to think about risk the way our parents and grandparents did. Risk, in the financial world today, is about losing opportunity, and there are four basic types of risk: credit, purchasing power, market, and financial.

1. **Credit Risk** is associated with fixed investments such as bank certificates of deposit, insurance company fixed accounts, or other accounts where you stand to lose some or all of your uninsured investment should the bank or institution fail.

2. **Purchasing Power Risk** is most often associated with bonds, which provide a more stable, reliable rate of return but rarely keep up with inflation and thus are poor vehicles for investment growth.

3. **Market Risk** is associated with stocks which, like dividend paying whole life insurance and real estate, does historically earn more than inflation but is subject to volatility from market forces.

Risk, in the financial world today, is about losing opportunity, and there are four basic types of risk: credit, purchasing power, market, and financial.

4. **Financial Risk** is assumed when you invest in an individual equity. Financial risk can be reduced by investing in multiple stocks through vehicles like mutual funds. But even in mutual funds we expose ourselves to market risk, so we reduce market risk by investing in multiple markets through diversification.

THE RISK OF LOST OPPORTUNITY

The investment industry tends to define risk as the chances your investment will decline—your risk of losing money. Risk is presented as the greatest foe of wealth creation. But the risk of any particular investment losing money pales compared with the risk of lost opportunity. In most cases, far more money is left on the table due to lost opportunity cost than to market or financial risk.

Lost Opportunity Cost is that part of your investment that stops working for you, and the earnings potential that loss represents. The most common example is taxes. Under the Lost Opportunity Cost concept, the money you pay in taxes is not just an expense, but it is money no longer able to work for you to earn more money. In Part V, "Making Sense of Insurance," you will learn about uncomplicated life insurance policies that are the safest place to invest, earn a competitive interest rate, and the income is untaxed.

Lost Opportunity Cost is that part of your investment that stops working for you, and the earnings potential that loss represents. The most common example is taxes.

But most investment portfolios are structured in such a way that they suffer from Lost Opportunity Costs. When we pay taxes on the interest and dividends we earn, those dollars no longer have earnings potential. Furthermore, the interest and dividends left over after paying taxes are often reinvested directly into the same CD, mutual fund, stock, or other vehicle that produces yet more taxable earnings. This is the vicious and expensive Lost Opportunity Cost Cycle, and it often begins with a misguided conviction that we are avoiding risk.

LOST OPPORTUNITY COST ILLUSTRATION

The charts on the next page illustrate the hypothetical growth of $100,000 invested in a vehicle paying a steady 6 percent annual return. At the end of the first year, the investment sends you a "thank-you" note–an IRS 1099 tax form showing you earned $6,000. In a 30 percent tax bracket, you owe $1,800, leaving a net profit of $4,200, or a real return of only 4.2 percent.

Minding the investment industry "rule" to never touch principal, most investors will roll over the full $6,000, and pay the $1,800 tax bill out of earnings or income that probably has itself been taxed at least once. They think they are making progress by building principal. That's faulty thinking. They are, instead, creating a compound tax problem, and a potentially huge lost opportunity cost.

Yes, our investor now has $106,000 in his or her account. But in addition to losing income on the $1,800 gone to taxes, there is now the additional income that would have been earned on the lost $1,800—$1,800 x 6%=$108.

The real cost is then $1,908 to earn $6,000. This phenomenon repeats itself year after year, compounding, growing your opportunity cost, lost to a taxable investment.

If you continued this way for twenty-five years, you would have accumulated $429,188 on your original investment. But what was the cumulative Lost Opportunity Cost of this strategy? The cost to accumulate this $429,188 was $193,135 lost to taxes and earnings on taxes.

How many examples can you think of in your own life, where money has ceased working for you?

 # The High Cost of Building Wealth: How Lost Opportunity Costs From Taxes Mount Up

$100,000 AT 6% RETURN FOR 30 YEARS, TAXED

	A 6% annual return/30% tax rate			Taxes paid + lost earnings on taxes paid			
	Beginning of Year Value	Assumed Earnings for the Year	Year End Value (Before Taxes)	Cumulative Taxes Paid Out-of-Pocket	Earnings Compounded on Taxes Paid Out-of-Pocket:	Cummulative Taxes & Lost Opportunity Cost:	Real return after taxes + lost opportunity cost
1st year:	100,000	6,000	106,000	1,800	108	1,908	104,092
2nd year:	106,000	6,360	112,360	3,708	337	4,045	108,315
3rd year:	112,360	6,742	119,102	5,730	701	6,431	112,670
4th year:	119,102	7,146	126,248	7,874	1,216	9,090	117,158
5th year:	126,248	7,575	133,823	10,147	1,897	12,044	121,779
10th year:	168,948	10,137	179,085	23,725	8,510	32,235	146,850
15th year:	226,090	13,565	239,656	41,897	22,810	64,707	174,949
20th year:	302,560	18,154	320,714	66,214	49,243	115,457	205,257
25th year:	404,893	24,294	429,187	98,756	94,378	193,134	**236,053**
30th year:	541,839	32,510	574,349	142,305	167,844	310,149	264,201

A CASE STUDY OF RISK AND EMOTIONAL RESPONSE

Whether it's on the playground, in our social lives, in our professions, in the teams or other groups we're attracted to, humans like to be where the action is. We stop and gawk at car wrecks, fires, a couple arguing on a street corner. We want to belong, have our opinions and choices validated, be on the winning side.

This instinct may have some genetic benefit in socializing us for mutual protection, but it is often a fatal flaw when it comes to investment. To illustrate how our feelings about risk drive us to make poor decisions about money, I've created an imaginary client who has given me a significant portfolio to manage for the next twenty-five years.

This client wants to invest aggressively because he's read that this is the way to make the most money in the shortest period of time, and he wants to retire young. As part of encouraging him to make wise choices, I explain how diversification works to build wealth over the long haul. I show him a chart that compares the long-term performance of various types of investments.

He sees that the best-performing investments over the preceding five or ten years were venture capital and small-capitalization stocks and instead of following my advice to spread his investments more broadly, he insists that I put all his money into those two categories. I can't talk him out of it so I do as he instructs.

Five Years Later:

I meet with my client to review his portfolio. He's expecting to have doubled his money, at least. Instead, his choices were now the worst-performing asset classes, losing more than 20 percent of his money. After he stops berating himself, he looks at a new chart of investment returns and sees that real estate has been doing very well. Real estate is a no-brainer, he tells me. It always goes up, right? Yes, I say, it does, but it's just one of a number of areas you could invest in to diversify.

But he wants to make up for his losses as quickly as possible, and besides, his friends at the country club are all bragging about how much they've made in real estate so it must be a good idea. He wants me to move the remaining 80 percent of his original portfolio (which has also lost buying power due to inflation) into real estate investment trusts.

Again I try to talk him out of putting all his eggs in one basket, but he's determined. "Just don't ever mention venture capital again," he chuckles.

...he wants to make up for his losses as quickly as possible, and besides, his friends at the country club are all bragging about how much they've made in real estate so it must be a good idea.

Ten Years Later:

I meet again with my client who is hopeful but less self-confident. He's disappointed to find that, yes, real estate went up, but not very much. His investments performed about the same as risk-free, plain vanilla bank certificates of deposit and money market funds.

> *Against my advice, he directs me to move his money all into the stock market.*

Once again, I show him a chart of all the different asset classes and he's chagrined to notice that while his money was essentially treading water, his old nemesis venture capital funds–which he'd sold five years earlier in disgust–was now one of the best-performing investments again. I reassure him that time is his friend, and encourage him to ride out the real estate market. Eventually it'll have its bull market.

But he's frustrated. He's read somewhere that the stock market always goes up 11 percent a year. His accountant told him that, so it must be true. Against my advice, he directs me to move his money all into the stock market.

Fifteen Years Later:

Most asset classes have risen in a fairly tight pattern, and did much better than inflation, including his stocks. He should be happy. But way out ahead of the field again is his old nemesis, venture capital. It's done twice as well as stocks. If he'd left his money in venture capital from the beginning, he'd have enough to retire. Instead, he's starting to feel desperate. He's not getting any younger and doesn't want to miss out on the hot trend so he tells me to move everything back into venture capital.

> *He's not getting any younger and doesn't want to miss out on the hot trend so he tells me to move everything back into venture capital.*

Twenty Years Later:

Getting grayer and growing nervous about retirement, my client is hoping to see his portfolio double. But he's dismayed to find that the hot corner in the market during the period was a relatively new asset category: international equities. He's ticked that he missed yet another boat and was left with mediocre returns from his venture capital investments. At least, he says, I didn't lose anything. It's a new global economy so, against my advice, he decides to move everything in international equities.

Twenty-Five Years Later:

My client wants to retire in five years. International investments have been one of the worst asset classes over the period and his portfolio failed to keep up with inflation. Panicked, terrified of losing what he has, he directs me to take all his money and park it in something absolutely safe, like bonds. "At least I'll know what I have, and I can sleep at night." I tell him about some alternative strategies, going back to our initial conversations about asset allocation and diversification. But he's been so badly burned, he insists I put everything into high-yield bonds.

Thirty Years Later:

Interest rates have risen, the price of his bonds dropped, and his investment was in one of the worst asset classes. Stocks ruled the day. He finally gets the message but now it's too late. By grasping at trends, allowing his fears to guide his choices, he has lost the opportunity to gain the financial independence he wanted in retirement.

By grasping at trends, allowing his fears to guide his choices, he has lost the chance to gain the financial independence he wanted in retirement.

INVESTMENT RETURNS VS. INVESTOR RETURNS

Between 1986 and 2005, the average return of the S&P 500 was 11.90 percent. But, according to Dalbar Inc., a leading financial-services research firm, the average ACTUAL returns of investors over the same time was a dismal 3.9 percent.* The difference was not caused by poor fund selection or onerous fees. It was caused by investors' emotional reactions driving their investment strategies. Stability, coupled with compounded returns, is the recipe for investment success.

Risk is not about losing money. Successful investing requires patience and discipline. Emotion and lack of under-standing of how markets work are the main causes of poor investment performance.

*(Source: Dalbar Inc.'s "Quantitative Analysis of Investor Behavior" Study Investors News June 12, 2006)

PART IV

The Real World of Real Estate

10 The Good, Bad, and Ugly of Real Estate

> ### The best investment on earth is earth.
> –Louis Glickman, prominent New York real estate investor

THE US CENSUS BUREAU reported in 2005 that 73.8 million Americans own their own homes. Owning a home is the linchpin of the American Dream and it can be a vehicle for wealth creation. But there are many misconceptions that unnecessarily limit the use of this unique financial tool.

How many of the following facts about real estate surprise you?

1. The return on equity is always zero.
2. Real estate growth is solely based on market value.
3. Equity is safer if it is separated from the property.
4. The less equity you have in your home the better off you'll be in hard times.
5. Home equity is not liquid.
6. Home equity is not safe.
7. Mortgage debt is good debt, so long as it's tax deductible.
8. Real estate leveraging enhances your return on investment.
9. Mortgage payments are not an expense; they support an asset.

MISCONCEPTIONS ABOUT REAL ESTATE

So many people think the ability to pay off their home mortgage is a sign of financial success. In a perfect world, investments are safe, guaranteeing a competitive return, easy to convert into cash, provide tax benefits, and allow the investor to control it. Many investors believe the only thing that meets these criteria is their home. This is Depression-era thinking, and it makes no financial sense.

DEBT CAN SET YOU FREE

The following example illustrates two different ways of managing a home asset valued at $500,000, and why one is far superior to the other. Homeowner "A" and Homeowner "B" own identical houses in the same neighborhood on the coast of Mississippi.

Homeowner "A" has worked hard and paid extra on his mortgage each month.

Now he owes nothing, and lives in a home with $500,000 in equity. He has no money in the bank, but he knows he has a place to live and an asset that will keep growing.

Homeowner "B" has also worked hard, but instead of paying down his mortgage, he made the minimum payments and saved as much of his earnings as he could.

Now he has $400,000 in cash assets. He still owes $400,000 on his mortgage, leaving him $100,000 in equity. He could pay off his mortgage with his cash assets, but he likes the feeling of having a fat rainy-day fund. If nothing else, he could make those mortgage payments for many years into the future.

> *One day, Hurricane Katrina comes through and flattens the whole neighborhood.*

Homeowner "A" and Homeowner "B" commiserate. They are in the same leaky boat. Their families are homeless, they've lost their income because the local economy was also washed away, and now they need to find shelter and the money to pay for it all.

Who comes out ahead?

Homeowner "A" goes to his bank confident that his $500,000 equity will seem very attractive as collateral for a loan. But there's no house anymore, just a scrap of swamp in an area that has just been proven to be an extremely dangerous place to build. The land's worth nothing if no one wants to buy it. And banks don't like lending to borrowers with no income. If he didn't need the money, they'd have given it to him right away.

Homeowner "A" had insurance, but he bought the cheapest policy he could find. The insurance company is less interested in making him whole than it is in generating the largest possible profit for its shareholders. So Homeowner "A" becomes embroiled in a long, drawn-out legal battle to get the insurance company to build him a new house.

A year passes and Homeowner "A" and his family are still living in a FEMA trailer waiting for the big check and eating peanut butter sandwiches.

Homeowner "B" also goes to the bank, but he doesn't need a loan. He's got $400,000 in his rainy day fund, and it sure did rain! He can relocate his family, buy another house, feed his family, and start anew.

Because he only had 20 percent equity, Homeowner "B"'s mortgage company required him to carry full insurance written to protect the bank's interest. That means Homeowner "B" has a powerful ally that will help make sure the insurance company meets its obligations. He has enough insurance to rebuild.

Even if Homeowner "B" didn't have proper insurance, he has the option of defaulting on his loan and letting the mortgage company take the swamp land he used to call home.

You don't need a Category 5 hurricane to make this illustration work the way it does.

> *A year passes and Homeowner "A" and his family are still living in a FEMA trailer waiting for the big check and eating peanut butter sandwiches.*

> *Homeowner "B" has a powerful ally that will help make sure the insurance company meets its obligations. He has enough insurance to rebuild.*

WHEN MORE IS LESS

Another misconception about real estate is that the more equity you have in your home, the safer the investment. It's partly true, but not for you. The more equity you have tied up in your property, the safer the risk is for the bank, and the greater the risk for you. I'll let my two homeowners illustrate again.

In this version of the example, both Homeowners "A" and "B," the wage earners in their families, have died in the hurricane. And instead of having his mortgage paid off, Homeowner "A" left his family with a $50,000 balance on his mortgage.

Widow "A," with no cash and only minimal disaster subsidies, can't shelter her family and make mortgage payments on swamp land while she waits for the insurance company check. So she goes to the mortgage company and points out that the family never missed a single payment all those years and asks for consideration.

The banker reads Widow "A" the mortgage note that says that when the mortgage is in default, the bank can take the property and sell it to pay off the remaining debt. A speculator buys the property cheap, the bank deducts the amount due, and Widow "A" gets a check for a fraction of the equity the family had built up in the destroyed home.

The paradox of real estate is that the lower your equity, the more likely you'll be able to hang on to your home in bad times.

Widow "B" goes to the same mortgage company, which is on the hook for her $400,000 mortgage, and asks the bank to work out some sort of payment plan she can afford. This time, the bank is happy to oblige. The value of the land would never cover the mortgage, so the bank's best chance to avoid losing money and maybe even continue to make a profit is to make it possible for Widow "B" to keep the loan current.

The paradox of real estate is that the lower your equity, the more likely you'll be able to hang on to your home in bad times.

A SHORT COURSE IN MORTGAGE HISTORY

One of the outcomes of the Great Depression that remains with us today are Social Security and the 30-year mortgage, and both are subject to broad misconceptions about their purpose and how they operate.

Prior to modern mortgage practices, the banking industry often made its money not on the interest or fees charged for a mortgage, but on the calculation that property owners would default and the banks would take ownership of the property. In modern parlance, this is known as "loan to own," and more than a few real estate fortunes were made by lenders during the Depression who turned over the same properties many times by approving borrowers they knew couldn't keep up the payments.

As the satirist and performer Will Rogers, *(right)*, observed at the time, "It's not politics that is worrying the country; it's the second payment."

Mortgages then were typically interest-only with a balloon payment, due in as little as five years. Borrowers who defaulted ended up with no equity. Fewer than four out of ten households owned their homes.

To alleviate the financial stresses of the times, the federal government developed a number of initiatives designed to help Americans deal with debt, jobless-ness, home ownership, and retirement. Programs like Social Security, unemploy-ment compensation, and the Federal Housing Administration (FHA) altered the way Americans viewed their jobs, pensions, and home ownership. The American Dream that we speak of today was born of these programs.

Today's looming Social Security crisis is evidence that these programs and the social ethos they spawned are seriously out of synch with reality. In fact, the Social Security Act was never intended to be the social program that most Americans understand it to be today. To reduce unemployment, the government needed to shrink the work force. Most Americans worked from high school until they became too old, too ill, or died. The Social Security Act provided a guaranteed income that encouraged workers to retire and helped remove a signifi-cant number of people from the workforce, thereby opening up job opportunities.

> *Today's looming Social Security crisis is evidence that these programs and the social ethos they spawned are seriously out of synch with reality.*

At the time, most Americans spent up to 40 percent of their earnings on shelter. This was leaching a lot of money out of the economy. The solution was the creation of the FHA, which reconstructed the way average Americans purchased and funded their homes. The FHA lowered the down payment requirements and imposed qualification standards based on a buyer's ability to repay the loan. The legislation required commercial banks and lenders to follow the FHA rules.

Some seventy years later, the premise on which these programs were based is obsolete: people no longer live out their entire lives in the same house and many families own more than one home; defined benefit pension plans are being replaced by defined contribution plans; consumers are more sophisticated investors; and the market provides more financing options.

In spite of changed economic circumstances, residual attitudes from the Depression continue to misinform our decisions and we need to develop a fresh approach.

11 Making Good Mortgage Choices

CLIENTS OFTEN ASK ME if they should pay off their mortgages in fifteen years instead of the traditional thirty. It's a question I enjoy answering because it gives me the chance to explain the concept of lost opportunity costs.

Every investment decision involves a choice about opportunity cost.

Simply put, a lost opportunity cost in investment is a missed opportunity to make money. The term is also used to describe lost manpower, manufacturing output, and any other finite, limited resource.

Lost opportunity cost is a major factor in hindering the creation of wealth. Studies suggest that 60 percent of potential investor wealth is lost to missed opportunities. Every investment decision involves a choice about opportunity cost.

THE WOULDA-COULDA-SHOULDA FACTOR

An investor buys $10,000 worth of ABC Co. stock. A year later, it's worth $10,500, a 5% return. He reads in the paper that he could have invested that $10,000 in a bank certificate with an annual yield of 6% which would have grown to $10,600. His lost opportunity cost was $100.

Lost opportunity costs are typically driven by emotion, personal comfort levels, or the desire for peace of mind. Putting money into safe and predictable bank CDs, for example, may make it easier to sleep at night but such a decision is almost always going to have an opportunity cost compared with other, more aggressive investments. Every time you choose between two courses of action, you assume the potential cost of the option not taken.

LOST OPPORTUNITY COST & MORTGAGE PAYMENTS

Real estate ownership is the key to wealth creation, but only if you manage the financial transaction with an eye toward opportunity costs. The principal elements of home ownership are:

1. Leverage. You use someone else's money to buy it.

2. Tax Benefits. Interest is deductible.

3. Shelter. It provides a necessity.

4. Quality of Life. It enhances your lifestyle.

5. Forced Savings. It is the number one way that most Americans create wealth.

By the time most of us pay off our home mortgages, we've paid more in interest than the purchase price. If you borrow $125,000 at 8 percent for thirty years, you'll pay more than $200,000 in interest on top of the $125,000 you borrowed. Your $125,000 house will have cost you $330,000.

FIFTEEN OR THIRTY YEARS?

The first question we ask is what role you want the home to play in your financial plan. Would you like to own your home free and clear before your kids start college? Before you retire? Or would you simply like to save a significant chunk of change over the life of your mortgage?

Many people mistakenly believe that a fifteen-year mortgage is much more costly on a cash-flow basis than a thirty-year. While the monthly payments are somewhat higher on a shorter mortgage, the interest rate is typically lower, which offsets some of the increase in the monthly payment.

Many people mistakenly believe that a fifteen-year mortgage is much more costly on a cash-flow basis than a thirty-year.

Most importantly, compared with a thirty-year mortgage, you pay less than half the interest over the life of the loan. For most people, this is the greatest opportunity they will ever have to save a large sum of money.

Could you achieve a better return by taking a thirty-year mortgage and putting the monthly difference into a savings account? Not likely, so long as bank CD rates and similar low-risk investments are yielding less than your mortgage interest rate. Besides, most people today will spend any money they save, rather than salting it away. And even if they do, they lose the interest deduction on their taxes. In the 28 percent tax bracket, that's a substantial lost opportunity cost.

ADVANTAGES OF A 15-YEAR MORTGAGE OVER A 30-YEAR MORTGAGE:

You build equity more quickly

You own your own home sooner

You pay less than half the interest cost

The interest rate is typically lower

The higher the prevailing interest rate on mortgage loans, the more dramatic the savings in a fifteen-year mortgage.

15 VS. 30-YEAR MORTGAGE ILLUSTRATION

	30-yr @ 8%	15-yr @ 7.5%
Loan Amount	$100,000	$100,000
Monthly Payment	$734	$927
Total Interest	$164,165	$66,862
Savings	0	$97,293

EVALUATING OPPORTUNITY COST

You can find many automated calculators on the Internet that will crunch these numbers for you to reflect your particular situation, and to tell you how much you might save by paying extra against principal each month. These calculations are helpful but they don't reflect any other factors in a homeowner's personal financial situation. To make a major decision about something as critical as a mortgage without taking into account your entire financial picture is foolish.

Over the past several years, many home buyers have opted for a fifteen-year mortgage because of the interest savings and the shortened period it takes to pay it off. In the process, they often fail to evaluate that mortgage decision in light of their plans for long-term investing, insurance needs, tax-planning, and other elements of their financial strategies. If the only way a home buyer can afford the higher monthly payment is by neglecting long-term investments, they may be better off in the long run taking the thirty-year mortgage with the lower payment and investing the difference.

This decision should incorporate all the following issues:

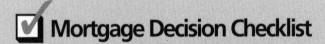 **Mortgage Decision Checklist**

1. Do you expect to remain in your home for the rest of your life?
2. Lost opportunity cost: could you get a better return elsewhere?
3. Have you maximized all other pretax, tax-deferred opportunities, such as 401(k), 403(b) deductions, IRA contributions?
4. Status of cash flow and other obligations such as auto loans, credit card debt, etc.
5. Job security.
6. Liquidity in your portfolio.
7. Your comfort with alternative investments (other than bank CDs).
8. Potential inheritance.
9. Outside investment opportunities.
10. Tax bracket and need for future deductions.
11. Future interest rates.
12. Your age.
13 Anticipated inflation rate over the term of the mortgage.
14. Future college, health care, or long-term care expenses.
15. Your personal spending and investment discipline.

Of all these issues, none is more important than the last–your saving discipline. People accumulate the bulk of their wealth in two areas: a retirement account, and home equity. The reason has nothing to do with rates of return on these investments. Instead, it's a question of human nature. We save when the savings are automatic.

We all have the best intentions but there's always a legitimate reason why we can't make that additional contribution to our savings account. A mortgage is simply a forced savings program–it's the first check we write every month. That's why the thirty-year mortgage is the best option for younger people, so long as the homebuyer has the discipline to follow through on the alternatives we will discuss later.

PAY IT OR INVEST IT?

Most people who intend to inhabit their homes for a lengthy time and whose instinct is to accelerate the payoff of their mortgages may be saving on their interest expense, but they may also be undermining their future security. As we demonstrated in the Katrina examples, the more important goal should be to create enough liquid (accessible cash) wealth to be sure you can make payments in the future.

It would seem common sense to pay down a mortgage and "earn" more by lowering interest cost than you'd earn putting that money into an equally risk-free bank CD instead.

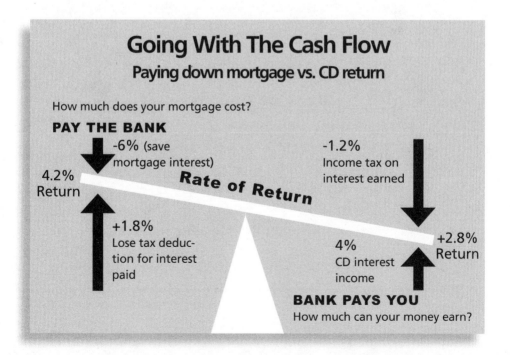

A BETTER WAY TO THINK

If you are an earner with an effective tax rate of 30 percent, the dollar you paid the bank in interest, or the dollar you put in the bank CD, has already been taxed once. You had to earn $1.43 for every dollar you paid against your mortgage, or put into the CD. That means 30 percent of every taxed dollar is no longer available to help you create wealth.

A key rule of investing: the longer you keep Uncle Sam out of your wallet, the more wealth you'll accumulate.

Assuming you plan to hold on to your home, instead you could take that pre-tax $1.43 and put all of it in a tax-deferred retirement plan that would give you funds to pay those mortgage payments in the future, when you retire. Investing those dollars in a fixed account would yield the same return as illustrated above, but the tax bite would be deferred, and you would in time be earning a rate of return on a larger amount of money.

A key rule of investing: the longer you keep Uncle Sam out of your wallet, the more wealth you'll accumulate.

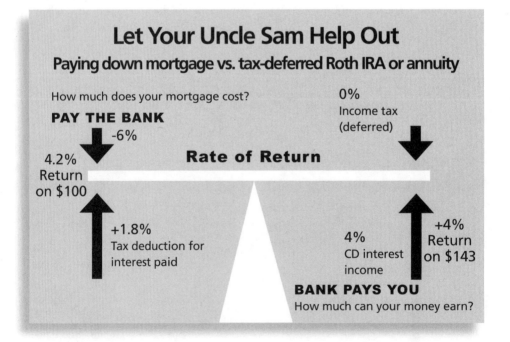

Let Your Uncle Sam Help Out
Paying down mortgage vs. tax-deferred Roth IRA or annuity

How much does your mortgage cost?

PAY THE BANK
-6%

4.2%
Return
on $100

Rate of Return

0%
Income tax
(deferred)

+1.8%
Tax deduction for
interest paid

4%
CD interest
income

+4%
Return
on $143

BANK PAYS YOU
How much can your money earn?

Paying your mortgage down may turn out to be an opportunity cost you'll pay for in retirement.

Even if you chose to put your after-tax dollars in investments that earn tax-free or tax-deferred income, the difference is small between the return you get from paying down your mortgage and the return you get by investing those dollars: 4.2 percent on your mortgage pay-down versus 4 percent from alternative investments. But your investments will be earning interest on interest, something your mortgage pay-down cannot achieve.

> *Paying your mortgage down may turn out to be an opportunity cost you'll pay for in retirement.*

WHAT'S THE BEST OPTION FOR YOU?

Interest saved is less important than interest lost—an opportunity cost. Thus, a fifteen-year mortgage may not be a good idea. By paying your home mortgage off faster, you are in effect removing a dollar that could be in your investment portfolio and instead locking it away where it can never earn another cent. Likewise, any dollar you pay in taxes will never find its way back into your portfolio.

This is what we mean when we say that paying your mortgage down ahead of time is, in effect, lending money to the bank at 0 percent interest. The bank turns around and, using its leverage, invests that dollar to work as hard as 10 dollars. Yes, you are saving interest expense, but that dollar can never again work for you as it could have if it was invested and allowed to grow.

The key factor in choosing a fifteen-year versus thirty-year is your personal savings discipline. If it's strong, the thirty-year option might be better. If not, the fifteen-year option could be for you.

The reason most wealth is created through retirement plans or home ownership is because it is the easiest decision to make, and the easiest commitment to keep. When you sign on to a retirement savings plan, you commit to writing two dozen or so checks a year. Over a thirty-year working career that's 780 checks all flowing from a single decision. When you buy a home with a thirty-year mortgage, you commit to writing 360 checks.

In my analysis, a fifteen-year mortgage may best suit the already wealthy. They will have maxed-out their deductibility of $1,000,000 on mortgage debt. They usually have plenty of accessible cash assets, would

> *...paying your mortgage down ahead of time is, in effect, lending money to the bank at zero percent interest.*

rather not bother writing that mortgage check every month, and it simplifies their estate for their heirs. But chances are good that if you're already wealthy you aren't reading this book.

If your mortgage decision is part of a complete and diversified financial plan, and you are starting your financial plan at a reasonably early age, the thirty-year mortgage allows you to consider investments that perform best over long periods of time. Each investor benefits from taking their own emotional responses into consideration when making such important choices.

MY FAVORITE OPTION

There is an investment vehicle that has been around for over 1,400 years that historically provides both the returns and risk comfort levels that is required for long-term wealth creation. It is the safest option, and it fulfills the essential ownership and control elements we discussed at the beginning of this journey.

It is the cash value component (not premiums paid) of old-fashioned, dividend-paying, participating whole life insurance. Only this kind of insurance provides a return similar to what banks offer, provides investment return guarantees, and, because you own this type of insurance contract, there are no anonymous shareholders in line ahead of you making a profit from your money.

There is no taxation on whole life earnings that are reinvested and distributions can be tax free if they are received as loans against the contract. We will go into much more detail about participating life insurance in later chapters. But here is how participating life contracts compare with paying down your mortgage.

If your mortgage decision is part of a complete and diversified financial plan, and you are starting your financial plan at a reasonably early age, the thirty-year mortgage allows you to consider investments that perform best over long periods of time.

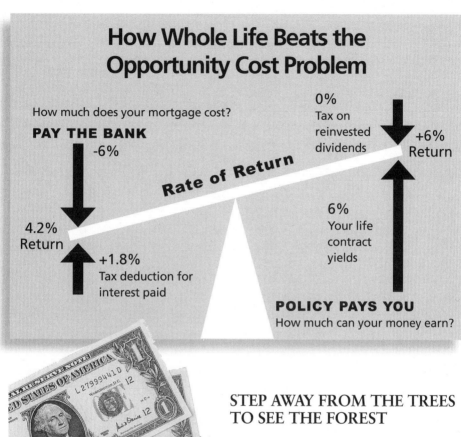

How Whole Life Beats the Opportunity Cost Problem

How much does your mortgage cost?

PAY THE BANK
-6%

Rate of Return

4.2%
Return
+1.8%
Tax deduction for
interest paid

0%
Tax on
reinvested
dividends

+6%
Return

6%
Your life
contract
yields

POLICY PAYS YOU
How much can your money earn?

STEP AWAY FROM THE TREES TO SEE THE FOREST

Homeowners need to consider their mortgage decisions in a much broader context than most investors realize. Just looking at monthly payments and interest rates is short-sighted.

One of the most common mistakes people make is tying up too much of their money in their homes. Your home should serve your financial goals, not the other way around.

12 Unlocking Hidden Wealth in Real Estate

> ### Wealth unused might as well not exist.
> *–Aesop, ancient Greek folk hero*

HOME OWNERSHIP IS OFTEN WORK—at least in terms of maintenance. What homeowner hasn't, at one time or another, had to wriggle into a dirty crawl space or root around a dingy basement to fix a leak or some other urgent repair?

As we live in our homes, we get to know them, what they were made from, and how they were constructed. We unlock little secrets in our homes–hidden newspapers in the attic with stories about the previous owners, or the ventilation system that wasn't put together properly and circulates air only on one level.

In addition to these day-to-day revelations, your home has a secret waiting to be discovered–hidden capital to be unlocked and exploited: your equity.

Real estate is a unique investment in this regard. Your home allows you to leverage the equity that you build in it, and enjoy the tax benefit of the interest deduction. These factors help make real estate a major component of most invest-ment portfolios. It can be one of the best invest-ments you possess, if you know how to manage it well and wisely.

LESSONS FROM THE MASTERS

You can employ the same concepts the tycoons do to enhance your investment portfolio with the purchase of your family home.

Real estate investing is like medicine, law, or any other field: you can learn from trial and error–often costly–or you learn from studying experts who have created billions of dollars of wealth in real estate.

You can employ the same concepts the tycoons do to enhance your investment portfolio with the purchase of your family home. The fundamentals apply whether the property is a Trump-sized tower in Manhattan or a starter Cape in the suburbs.

The average homeowner has been led to believe that equity equals wealth. Nothing could be further from the truth. Equity is actually a cost. Professional real estate investors call equity an opportunity cost because it is the capital they have to put up–take out of their investment portfolios–to control a piece of real estate. The rest comes from financing.

The pros put a great deal of energy into minimizing how much capital they have to commit to control property, not because they don't have it but because it makes more sense to use someone else's money to create wealth.

Consider the following example:

You purchase a home for $500,000 with a down payment of $100,000. After five years, the value of the home has increased to $700,000 and you have paid the mortgage principal down from $400,000 to $300,000. If you sell, you'll net a pre-tax, pre-commission profit of $300,000.

Suppose, instead, you had opted for an interest-only mortgage. Rather than paying down $100,000 of principal and "building" equity, you invested that $100,000 in an investment that yielded a return of 8 percent. After five years, your investment would have grown to almost $150,000. When you sell both the home and the investment, your equivalent pre-tax, pre-commission profit is now almost $350,000.

…no asset provides quite the leverage and safety of real estate.

In other words, if your money can earn more than the cost of your debt, paying down equity will not increase your wealth. There is, in the example above, an "opportunity cost" of paying down mortgage principal. When you add in the huge tax incentive of the interest deduction, the after-tax cost of the loan can be very low.

That is what we mean when we talk about leveraging an asset, and no asset provides quite the leverage and safety of real estate.

COST OF CAPITAL VERSUS USE OF CAPITAL

Real estate professionals strive to build equity in a project, and then leverage that equity to take advantage of another opportunity, thus becoming their own bank. They borrow against the equity in their projects at one rate, and invest in projects that have higher projected rates of return.

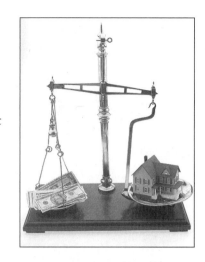

If Donald Trump can get a mortgage on Building A at a cost of 5 percent after taxes, and can invest in a new project that makes 10 percent per year after taxes, he has created wealth using other people's money. Furthermore, he enjoys the additional benefit of Building A's market value rising over time. This is how banks make money as well, paying you a low interest rate for your deposits and then using your money to make loans at a higher rate. The bank is also using other people's money, but you are the other people.

WHEN IS LEVERAGING A GOOD BET?

Leveraging your real estate equity can be a very effective way to build your investment portfolio but it is not always the best option. Homeowners must be realistic and honest about their investment goals, and their ability to exercise discipline in their investment strategies. As long as you have the discipline to invest the extra money you borrow rather than fritter it away on luxuries, you're likely to come out ahead.

Homeowners must be realistic and honest about their investment goals, and their ability to exercise discipline in their investment strategies.

During periods like the current one, when mortgage rates are historically low, it is likely you can earn more by using your equity to take advantage of other opportunities, even prosaic investments like tax-deferred IRAs or 401(k)s. The pre-tax rate of return can equal or exceed the post-tax cost of the mortgage. The key is to put your liberated home equity into a fixed or guaranteed account.

When should you consider real estate leveraging?

1. If you are reasonably confident that the expected benefit will exceed the net cost of the mortgage debt, after taking into account taxes and tax savings, and without assuming additional risk.

2. If you can create additional cash flow that will allow you to place additional funds into a retirement program or other investment vehicle for the purpose of accumulating additional assets earmarked to cover future mortgage payments.

3. If, by utilizing the tax deduction benefits on mortgage debt, you can offset the tax bite on a mandatory retirement plan distribution.

4. If you want to convert your non-deductible debt to tax-deductible debt to free up funds for use in attaining other financial planning goals.

5. If you want to address estate tax concerns by reducing income tax liability on tax-deferred assets.

AN EXAMPLE OF A 15-YEAR EQUITY STRATEGY

Tom and Alicia Home-owner own a well-kept home valued at $450,000 in a prosperous, stable neighborhood. They have been paying down their mortgage, and now have $250,000 in equity. They are comfortable, but they feel an urgency to accelerate their investment strategy.

The Homeowners decide to refinance with a 5.75 percent mortgage. They pay off the original note and now have unlocked their $250,000 in equity. They know better than to squander that hard-earned quarter-million dollars on a new boat or a fancy vacation. Instead they invest the money in a solid, guaranteed investment that yields 7 percent over the next fifteen years.

Fifteen years later, Tom and Alicia still own their beloved home. They've made all their mortgage payments on time. Meanwhile, the $250,000 in equity has been chugging along, earning 7 percent, and is now nearly $700,000.

If you deduct their mortgage payments during the same fifteen-year period—about $250,000—and the remaining unpaid principal of $175,000, and then add in the tax savings from the interest deduction of nearly $50,000, the Homeowners have increased their net worth by nearly $300,000. They still own their home, and the value of the property has doubled.

Just like real estate developers, the Homeowners were able to capitalize on the difference between the cost of capital and the use of capital.

Using real estate leveraging, Tom and Alicia created wealth while simultaneously protecting their home. Just like real estate developers, the Homeowners were able to capitalize on the difference between the cost of capital and the use of capital.

THE COMFORTS OF HOME EQUITY

Leveraging your home, for some people, is an unacceptable risk. Others may decide they are too undisciplined to make the commitment to keep the home equity in investments. They may be too tempted to squander it on luxury items. Real estate leveraging can be effective, if it is part of a larger investment structure you're prepared to stick with for the long haul.

Your personal comfort level should dictate the program or strategy you choose. If you decide to pursue real estate leveraging, the plan you choose to implement should include a transfer of risk that:

Your personal comfort level should dictate the program or strategy you choose.

1. Adjusts other elements of your investment portfolio (such as retirement assets).

2. Helps protect your hidden equity from market risk.

3. Shifts assets eligible for capital gains taxes from tax deferred accounts (retirement accounts) to taxable accounts (mortgages) where tax deduction benefits can be realized.

Used in combination, these steps should help assure that your principal is safe, and your overall portfolio has utilized the tax code to its ultimate efficiency.

13 The Mortgage vs. Insurance Match-Up

> If the highest aim of a captain
> were to preserve his ship,
> he would keep it in port forever.
> –St. Thomas Aquinas, 13th century theologian

THE GREAT DEPRESSION caused more than 10,000 banks to fail, wiping out the life savings of millions. Corporations and governments defaulted on their debt, rendering their bonds worthless. The stock market decline pulled more than $800 billion of wealth (in 2005 dollars) out of the economy. An entire generation (or two) was scarred by the experience of the 1930s and those scars still inform many of our investment choices today.

What few people know, and isn't taught in our schools, is that the insurance industry was one of the few sectors of the economy that survived the Great Depression. It remained one investment that kept its promises.

As described earlier, I'm not speaking of the vast majority of insurance products being offered today. I'm speaking of an old, reliable form of insurance which is issued by mutually-owned companies in which you are the owner and the policyholder, earns a tax-free dividend, has cash value (like home equity) you can borrow against, and is about the safest investment on the planet.

What few people know, and isn't taught in our schools, is that the insurance industry was one of the few sectors of the economy that survived the Great Depression.

You won't hear many investment advisors and other professionals talk much about this kind of life insurance, sometimes called participating life, because most of them are being paid high commissions to sell you the other kind, written by companies owned by stockholders. The principal goal of publicly-held insurance companies is to make money on your premium payments to reward the stockholders. You are a customer, not an owner. In a mutual insurance company, you become an owner when you buy a policy.

> *The principal goal of publicly-held insurance companies is to make money on your premium payments to reward the stockholders.*

Participating whole life insurance contracts didn't exactly fall out of fashion. In the 1990s some sharp-eyed investment bankers discovered they could make a great deal of money by encouraging mutual policyholders to sell their ownership and convert these mutuals to stock-owned companies. Once public, the converted companies needed to satisfy the expectations of their investors so they began to invent all sorts of new products they could sell and make a profit on. The trend took off and today upwards of eighty percent of insurance companies are public.

COMFORTABLE VS. UNCOMFORTABLE TRANSACTIONS

Suppose you needed money and you could borrow against the equity in your home but instead of paying interest to the bank, you paid it to yourself? That is one of the best features of participating whole life, and one of the least understood. A home builds equity and these insurance policies build what's called cash value. You can borrow against equity or cash value, but the bank makes you go through a credit approval process to borrow against your home, whereas you can borrow against the cash value in your insurance policy with guaranteed approval. Furthermore, the interest on your insurance loan is credited back to you as the policy owner. The interest you pay to the bank belongs to the bank. You get no further benefit.

Buying a life insurance policy is one of those transactions that produces a fair amount of second guessing. There is often the fear that you've made a mistake, and the suspicion that goes along with having been "sold" something. Buying a home and getting a mortgage doesn't feel like that. You "buy" a mortgage, it isn't sold to you. The mortgage is connected to a tangible asset that you see every day, provides you with shelter, comfort, and security.

...you should by now begin to understand more clearly why, unless you own a bank, you shouldn't be relying on a bank to help you reach your goals.

An insurance policy is a piece of paper that promises some benefit in the future, after you're dead. Buying life insurance is one of those transactions we think of as an investment in somebody else's future–our heirs. Participating whole life does provide that protection, but it also can play a major role in creating wealth while you're still alive.

A participating whole life policy offers benefits such as long-term care, disability insurance, and a guaranteed return on your investment. Bank deposits are insured in much the same way as insurance contracts. But when you put your money in the bank, only the deposit is guaranteed–the return is not.

Like all life insurance, participating insurance contracts provide security for your beneficiaries, whether they be family or charities, and give you peace of mind. But they also offer the potential to enhance income, are a safe way to save, and the returns are similar to interest rates on thirty-year mortgages, but without the taxation.

If you've been reading from the beginning, you should by now begin to understand more clearly why, unless you own a bank, you shouldn't be relying on a bank to help you reach your goals.

Comfortable versus Uncomfortable Transactions

LIFE INSURANCE is often a **more comfortable** transaction

Benefits:
Death benefit
Long-term care
Disability
Guaranteed
Income
Tax Benefits

To unlock equity, you either:
Surrender policy
Borrow against cash value

Other factors:
- Loan approval guaranteed
- You get interest back
- Cash value, death benefit is collateral up to loan amount

A MORTGAGE is often a **less uncomfortable** transaction

Benefits:
Shelter
Security
Safe
Tangible
Growth
Tax Benefits

To unlock equity, you either:
Sell home
Borrow against equity

Other factors:
- Need bank approval
- Bank earns interest
- Entire home is collateral

CHOOSING REALITY OVER COMFORT

As people approach retirement age, they need to determine how much income they can expect from their investments and savings, without dipping into principal. Using an insurance policy as the place to park equity in your financial planning, you have the ability to put your assets to work now, and leave your heirs more money when you die.

Participating whole life policies pay holders dividends that are untaxed if reinvested. With the compounding effect of interest, these tax benefits increase the longer you own the policy. The cash value of your life insurance is protected from creditors, and it is held in a contract guaranteeing that the policy holder's intentions are met at the time of death.

We all understand the concept of borrowing against home equity, but clients are often confused about how they can access the cash value in their life policies. There are two options, and common misunderstandings about how they differ often leads to confusion and poor choices.

In much the same way that you can sell your home and get access to your equity, the life insurance policy can be surrendered, and you get your cash value. But selling a home involves significant costs, starting with the agent's commission and a host of other expenses and fees that come out of your pocket.

So why isn't everyone buying participating whole life? Besides not being exposed to it by insurance salespeople, there is a residual suspicion about insurance loans that emerged in the late 1970s, when interest rates were soaring and money markets funds–CDs, and so on–were paying as much as 15 percent. This was a huge inversion from the norm, when savings account interest rates were always the lowest.

At the time, whole life insurance policies were earning at most 8 percent. Insurance policy owners looking to tap into their cash value were told they could borrow against the policy but they were put off by the fact that they had to pay interest on their own money.

What they didn't understand was that interest paid does not go to stockholders of the insurance company. Rather, the interest

Using an insurance policy as the place to park equity in your financial planning, you have the ability to put your assets to work now, and leave your heirs more money when you die.

In much the same way that you can sell your home and get access to your equity, the life insurance policy can be surrendered, and you get your cash value.

ultimately comes back to you because you are borrowing your own money. You can choose whether to pay it back with interest only, or with principal and interest. But any payback of principal or interest will be placed right back into your insurance contract.

Investing money in a whole life insurance policy is one of the oldest and safest forms of economic security in the world.

Perhaps because of the tangible and useful nature of real estate, many people feel more comfortable borrowing against home equity even though it may be a poor choice. The typical family pays interest to the bank on the same dollar four or five times during their life because, although they have accumulated equity in their home, they put their money into an account that they don't control, is not liquid, and they could lose (through foreclosure) in bad times.

Investing money in a whole life insurance policy is one of the oldest and safest forms of economic security in the world. Ignore it and you will pay a hidden and unnecessary opportunity cost. See Part V, "Making Sense of Insurance," for greater detail about the advantages of insurance and how it works.

14 Mortgage Types and How to Use Them

> *A prince who will not undergo the difficulty of understanding must undergo the danger of trusting.*
> —*George Savile, 17th century English statesman*

THE FOUNDATION OF OUR ECONOMY is choice. When it comes to mortgages, lenders unceasingly come up with new creative ways to make money by financing real estate. The array of options is mind-bending, confusing, and so difficult to comprehend that many borrowers simply give up and take what they're offered.

Even the press can't figure it out. The financial pages and pundits have beaten it into our heads that the interest-only mortgage is a disaster waiting to happen. When interest rates go up, we've been told the world will come to an end because no one will be able to make their mortgage payments and the economy will collapse.

During this debate I cannot recall seeing a single writer or commentator who dared to educate consumers about the financial benefits of alternative mortgage products over conventional mortgages.

HOW TIMES HAVE CHANGED

Before the banking reforms triggered by the Crash of 1929 and the Great Depression, mortgage lending was almost exclusively on an interest-only basis with a balloon principal payment at the end of five or so years. Banks in those days "loaned to own:" they got all their profit (interest income) up front and when the big balloon payment came due, often got to take the property back and resell it, writing a new mortgage in the process.

Too many consumers don't bother to shop for a mortgage using the same skills and consideration they use when investigating any other transaction.

Today it is almost a religious belief that the 20 percent down, thirty-year amortization mortgage is the only smart option available when buying a home. Too many consumers don't bother to shop for a mortgage using the same skills and consideration they use when investigating any other transaction. This is a choice driven purely by emotion–when people find the home they want to live in, they will trust anyone willing to give them the money to purchase it.

Unlike most other financial transactions, when entering into a mortgage, the average consumer doesn't feel that he or she has been "sold" something. Rather, he feels he has been "given" something, and acts out of desperation rather than negotiation.

This thinking during the mortgage process is a result of underwriting–the process of proving to the bank that you don't need the money, that you can make payments. Thus many consumers feel they have to prove themselves to their banker, rather than the other way around.

The process of getting a mortgage has gotten dramatically more complex over the years. Factors such as points, prepayment penalties, miscellaneous costs, conventional versus jumbo financing, as well as the new credit-score system, all make mortgage choices a nightmare for the poorly-informed.

The process of getting a mortgage has gotten dramatically more complex over the years.

Mortgage companies, using the credit score of the applicant, now can charge different rates to different clients based on those scores. Mortgage lenders now can tell a potential client that they would be happy to match the low-low advertised rate in the paper, if only the client had a higher credit score.

WHICH MORTGAGE IS RIGHT FOR YOU?

Financing a home used to be like ordering from a menu with one item on it. Today, lenders offer hundreds of mortgage products with creative terms. You can pay the interest only for a few years, choose your monthly payment, or even close on your home with a "No Doc" (minimal income proof) mortgage. Which mortgage you choose should depend on the length of time you think you'll be in your home and your other financial obligations.

Which mortgage you choose should depend on the length of time you think you'll be in your home and your other financial obligations.

Conventional Thirty-Year Amortization Mortgage: Designed for the conventional family that anticipates living in their home for decades, these offer stable rates and long-term tax advantages. In the agrarian society that made up much of the US years ago, owning the family homestead provided for future generations. Today we view real estate as a financial investment as well as shelter, and we tend to think of the shelter as a temporary resting spot on the way to bigger, better, or more convenient residences in the future. And if we don't like the interest rate, there are dozens of lenders out there who will be happy to help us refinance—collecting fees and commissions each time. Mortgage options have changed to meet the new consumer's needs, but the consumer is still thinking in the past.

Fifteen- and Twenty-Year Mortgages: Shorter-term variations of the conventional thirty-year option, they usually have a slightly lower interest rate, higher monthly cost, and lower long-term tax benefits. This type of mortgage is a better option for any individual that can afford to ignore lost opportunity cost on money, as discussed previously. Most borrowers will come out ahead by taking the extra money you'd plow into mortgage payments and invest it in something else.

Adjustable Rate Mortgage Alternatives (ARM): These follow the traditional thirty-year amortization schedule, and are offered most commonly in shorter terms. The shorter the term, the lower the starting interest rate. During the term, your initial interest rate is guaranteed, but then the rate can change, subject to an annual cap or increase that is usually about 2 percent above the initial rate. The rate subsequently adjusts at regular intervals in accordance with current interest rate conditions. A 5/1 ARM, for example, has a fixed rate for five years and then adjusts every year for the next twenty-five years.

ARMs are attractive for buyers who anticipate moving within ten or so years from the time of the initial mortgage. Even with a potential interest rate increase, it's possible to calculate where the breakeven point is: where the higher fixed rate starts to cost more than the savings accrued during the early years of the loan. If a buyer anticipates moving or refinancing prior to this break-even date, an adjustable rate mortgage can be attractive.

ARM's can be particularly useful for consumers if the buyer is disciplined enough to save or invest the money left over from the lower mortgage payments in the early years of the loan. This discipline is necessary to set aside the funds to cover any future increases in the loan payments. Adding to these benefits, if interest rates happen to fall, ARM loans can actually save buyers money through lower interest rates in the future.

Finally, if a buyer has other significant expenses early on in the mortgage, such as college tuition, an adjustable rate mortgage can be a better option than incurring other nondeductible debt in order to meet anticipated shortfalls.

ARM's can be particularly useful for consumers if the buyer is disciplined enough to save or invest the money left over from the lower mortgage payments in the early years of the loan.

A COMPARATIVE EXAMPLE

A home buyer can get current average rates for a 30-year fixed, a 15-year fixed, and a 5/1 adjustable rate mortgage, and compare the numbers. For illustration purposes, let's assume you need a $200,000 mortgage.

Let's say the 30-year fixed rate is 6.62 percent, yielding a monthly payment of $1,280. The interest you pay over the life of this loan will total $260,786.

A 15-year fixed rate will be less. At 5.94 percent, your monthly payment would be $1,681. The interest you pay over the life of this loan will total $102,623, a saving over the 30-year of $158,163.

With a 5/1 ARM at 4.20%, your monthly payment will be $978 for the first five years. The total interest you pay over the life of the loan, if you stay in your home past five years, is anyone's guess because your rate will then adjust annually. But if you move after five years, that won't be an issue.

The average homeowner currently moves every seven years.

(Source: Coldwell Banker)

INTEREST-ONLY MORTGAGES

All mortgages are made up of two parts: one part goes toward the principal, which is your money. The other part goes toward the interest. Separating these two can allow you to create significant wealth if you understand how it works. The wealth comes from capturing money that is usually lost to opportunity costs.

The option to pay interest only lasts for a specified period, usually five to ten years. Borrowers have the right to pay more than interest if they want to. If the borrower exercises the interest-only option every month during the interest-only period, the payment will not include any repayment of principal. The result is that the loan balance remains unchanged.

For example, if a thirty-year loan of $100,000 at 6.25 percent is interest only, the monthly payment is $520.83 instead of $615.72 for a fully amortizing payment that would retire the loan over the term if the rate stayed the same. The difference in payment of $94.88 is principal which reduces the balance.

Interest-only mortgages are offered in many forms, the most common being five-, seven-, ten-, or thirty-year.

One of the benefits of these mortgages is that any payments applied to principal reduce the monthly payment, and can be paid at any time. On most interest-only loans, whether fixed or adjustable rate, the monthly mortgage payment will decline in the month following an extra payment. This is the only type of mortgage that offers this feature. On a conventional fixed rate mortgage, the payment never changes while on ARMs, the payment doesn't change until the next rate adjustment–five years for the first, and annually thereafter.

Interest-only loans are especially attractive for the self-employed or sales people who may have fluctuating income, but expect to earn a high annual income due to year-end bonuses. When cash flow is tight, they can afford the payment, and when they are flush they can make a one-time lump sum payment to principal, reducing their future mortgage obligation and giving them further control of their finances.

One of the benefits of these mortgages is that any payments applied to principal reduce the monthly payment, and can be paid at any time.

Interest rates are usually higher on these types of loans–typically .50 percent higher than the conventional thirty-year mortgage. But interest-only loans offer other substantial benefits for the smart mortgage consumer. They have much lower monthly payments, freeing up liquid cash for other financial opportunities. And the entire payment can be tax deductible, if the mortgage holder is disciplined enough to stash the extra money in a pre-tax retirement account, Roth IRA, or participating life insurance contract. These options open up opportunity to the interest-only mortgage holder for creating far greater wealth and keeping greater control of his or her financial destiny.

The payments you make against the principal on your mortgage loan are a cash deposit into a zero percent bank account that the bank gets to use for its profit-making purpose.

The payments you make against the principal on your mortgage loan are a cash deposit into a zero percent bank account that the bank gets to use for its profit-making purpose.

BEWARE THE UPSIDE-DOWN MORTGAGE TRAP

You may be one of the millions who have seen an ad or received a mailing offering a mortgage rate of 1.95 percent. This is the kind of mortgage option the press should be warning consumers about, instead of interest-only mortgages.

Although I have personally taken advantage of these loans from time to time, the average buyer is unaware of the implications of what they are actually getting into. They can be wonderful financial tools for people who really understand them. They can also be danger traps for consumers who don't do their homework.

What they don't understand is that their payment may be based on a 2 percent rate but their interest rate changes monthly based on a publicly-quoted index, such as the London Inter-Bank Cost of Funds Index (LIBOR) or the Moving Treasury Index (MTA).

This is the kind of mortgage option the press should be warning consumers about, instead of interest-only mortgages.

The trouble with these types of mortgages is that, in some cases, the borrower's minimum payment rate is not even covering the interest, which means they are, in effect, paying interest on unpaid interest. Many borrowers are surprised to learn they have gotten an upside down mortgage.

But these mortgages have a legitimate use for people who understand them, especially entrepreneurs or business owners, as well as people with significant equity in their home and income that may spike in the future. With negative accumulated interest on the loan, they can chose what year to pay the interest and control their tax deduction while reducing the dreaded Alternative Minimum Tax.

You can win at the mortgage game if you invest the time to understand each option.

Entrepreneurs seeking to finance their business venture will also use this type of loan. Most bankers will not lend to a business on a good idea or a good business plan. Whether the borrower is established with the lender or not, bankers usually require an asset for collateral. The most common asset put up to guarantee a business loan is the owner's equity in a home.

For individuals that have to pledge their personal assets to satisfy a corporate loan, LIBOR or MTA loans provide a much lower cost of funds than the prime rate and far greater payment control.

You can win at the mortgage game if you invest the time to understand each option.

Mortgage Pros and Cons

30-YEAR FIXED

Advantages:
- The monthly payment amount is lower than a 15-year loan.
- Payments can be easier to bear in the face of repair expenses or financial difficulties.

Disadvantages:
- Longer payment period and costs.

15-YEAR FIXED

Advantages:
- Own your home in half the time.
- Total interest cost is less than on a 30-year loan.

Disadvantages:
- The monthly payment is larger.
- Qualification may be difficult.

ADJUSTABLE RATE MORTGAGE (ARM)

Advantages:
- Initial rate can be 2-3 % lower than a fixed-rate mortgage.
- Homeownership is initially more affordable.
- Qualifying is easier
- When interest rates go down, payments go down.

Disadvantages:
- When interest rates go up, payments go up.

HYBRID, CONVERTIBLE ADJUSTABLE RATE MORTGAGES

Advantages:
- Blends the benefits of an ARM with the ability to convert to a fixed-rate mortgage.

Disadvantages:
- If you don't convert, it's a regular ARM.
- If interest rates are at a higher level when it's time to convert, you're stuck.

INTEREST-ONLY LOAN

Advantages:
- Borrowers can get a bigger loan, more house.
- Good for homebuyers who receive the bulk of their income in bonuses.
- Good for borrowers who big income increases soon.
- Good for borrowers who expect to move before the principal comes due.

Disadvantages:
- At end of the fixed period, you must refinance, pay a lump sum, or start paying on the principal.
- Borrowers must budget wisely to make lump sum payments.
- If the house doesn't appreciate, you may owe money at sale time.

OPTION ADJUSTABLE RATE MORTGAGES (ARM)

Advantages:
- Low initial minimum payments and up to four payment options, from a small minimum payment to a fully amortized payment.
- You choose the amount you want to pay.

Disadvantages:
- You can end up owing more than your original loan balance if you opt to pay less than the full interest charge; the difference will be added to your loan amount.

LOW OR NO DOCUMENT LOAN

Advantages:
- Designed for borrowers who have trouble verifying income, such as the self-employed, commissioned professionals, or service industry professionals.
- The lender does not require proof of income and assets.

Disadvantages:
- Interest rates are higher because of the higher risk.
- Larger down payments required.
- Credit standards may be higher.

BALLOON MORTGAGE

Advantages:
- Can be good for those who don't expect to own their homes past the date the balloon payment is due.
- Payments are usually lower than on conventional fixed loans.
- Can be a good choice if the home is expected to appreciate.
- Lower interest rate than long-term loan.

Disadvantages:
- After a few years, you must sell your house or refinance because all remaining principal is due. Interest rates may be much higher.
- You may end up owing the remaining principal plus additional settlement costs if the house doesn't appreciate.

FHA MORTGAGE

Advantages:
- The down payment is lower.
- The down payment can be borrowed from a relative.
- Loan rates are often lower.
- Qualification is easier.

Disadvantages:
- Loan amounts are capped.
- Processing may take longer.
- Appraisal guidelines may be stricter.
- Mortgage options are fewer.

HOW TO COMPARE MORTGAGE RATES

Cell phone companies, when they introduce new phones or when customers want to upgrade, offer you free or cheap prices on phones as long as you commit to a multi-year contract with an expensive escape fee if you want to terminate early.

The same kind of hook applies to your mortgage. Most people enter a mortgage arrangement with the mindset that the mortgage company is doing them a favor. They fail to understand that they are negotiating a financial deal and they have power in certain areas to get a better deal. Here are some areas that are negotiable when shopping for a mortgage.

WHAT TO NEGOTIATE WHEN MORTGAGE SHOPPING

Most people enter a mortgage arrangement with the mindset that the mortgage company is doing them a favor. They fail to understand that they are negotiating a financial deal and they have power in certain areas to get a better deal.

Points: Points generally fall into two categories, origination fees and discount fees. Discount fees are prepaid interest that a borrower elects to pay up front to buy down the interest rate on mortgage. For every point paid, the interest rate on a mortgage decreases by 1/8 percent. An origination fee is a fancy name for a sales commission used to compensate the broker for his role in the transaction. Both discount fees and loan origination fees paid will reduce the interest rate.

A loan that offers no points simply means you will be paying a higher interest rate on your mortgage. Points are deductible for income tax purposes. They are 100 percent deductible in the year you buy the home, and if you pay points on a refinance, they are deductible over the life of the loan. Most people forget that if you refinance any points that you have not deducted on a previous loan, you can deduct in the year of refinance.

For example, on a $300,000 loan, a point paid–$3000–is deductible the year you purchased the home. But if you were refinancing an existing loan, you could deduct only $100 a year for thirty years. Let's say that in the fifth year, you refinance again. Then you can deduct the $2,500 that had not been deducted from the previous loan.

Whether or not to pay points and buy down the interest rate is governed by the amount of time you plan to spend in the home and the type of mortgage you choose. A good rule of thumb is to pay points when you anticipate keeping the loan for a long term. If you anticipate refinancing in the near future, paying fewer points may be more attractive. You have to do the math to come up with right solution for your financial plans.

Prepayment Penalties: The latest surprise to creep into the mortgage business is the prepayment penalty. Prepayment penalties are similar to surrender charges found in a B-share mutual fund or an annuity contract. These penalties are beginning to resurface as a common part of the mortgage process so that the bank has a way of covering their cost of paying the broker that originated the loan if the loan doesn't stay on the books for the required earn-out period, typically two to three years.

These penalties can be "soft" or "hard." A soft penalty is only imposed if you refinance, not if you sell. A hard prepayment penalty is imposed unless you buy a new home and place the new mortgage with the same mortgage company.

Penalties are sometimes negotiated into the rates or the points.

Title and Escrow Fees: These insure that the mortgager has clear title to the property. Typically both owner's title insurance and lender's title insurance are issued by title insurance companies. These contracts protect both the buyer and lender, insuring a clear chain of title, guaranteeing that the persons conveying the property have the legal right to do so.

For refinances, this is a frustratingly unnecessary expense since you have already paid for this service when you initially bought your home. The best you can hope for is to pay only for the lender's side of the title insurance contract, and negotiate with your closing attorney or title company for a reduced rate for a reissue.

"Garbage" Fees: These are miscellaneous fees, ranging from $600 to $800. They are sometimes referred to as garbage fees since everything not otherwise accounted for in the mortgage fee can be dumped into them. These fees include such items as underwriting fee, processing fee, administrative fee, document preparation fee, funding fee, credit check fee, notarization courier fee, wire and tax service fee, flood certification fee, and so on.

CONCLUSION

Mortgage options have changed dramatically in recent years, and those who have the time and inclination will do well to research every aspect until they are satisfied they know what the stakes are.

For the rest of us whose time is tapped out, having a good relationship with a trusted mortgage broker can be just as profitable. Brokers have the ability to constantly shop for the best possible deal between multiple lenders. Since mortgage rates and terms change daily, working with someone you trust and establishing a good relationship can make a big difference.

Buying a mortgage should be treated like any other financial transaction. Shopping for the best deal can pay off in the end.

PART V

Making Sense of Insurance

15 All Insurance Is Not Created Equal

> *Something unpleasant is coming when men are anxious to tell the truth.*
> *–Benjamin Disraeli, 19th century English statesman*

EVERY TIME YOU PUT YOUR MONEY to work making money, you've made an investment. Every investment has two principal elements that every investor ponders, consciously and often not, before committing his or her money. Is the risk worth the potential reward? In most instances, the higher the risk, the greater the potential return, and vice versa.

There is no such thing as a zero-risk place to put your money because risk is a function of time, and time is unceasing–if you are standing still you are by definition moving backward. Even getting currency out of an automatic teller machine carries risk, however infinitesimal. A pick-pocket might steal your wallet. An international crisis could cause a panic that makes your dollars worth less before you have a chance to spend them.

A bank CD is about as close as we get to a zero risk investment. The highest-risk investments are the most speculative. In the 1980s some wealthy Texas oilmen speculated in silver to such an extent that they ended up owning a significant percentage of the world's avail-

> *There is no such thing as a zero-risk place to put your money because risk is a function of time, and time is unceasing–if you are standing still you are by definition moving backward.*

able silver. It was a huge risk and they made an out-sized reward–hundreds of millions of dollars overnight. Then, they just as quickly lost every penny.

> *Evaluating risk and managing it is what successful investors and investment professionals do best.*

The ideal investment is the one that pays the most for the least amount of risk. Evaluating risk and managing it is what successful investors and investment professionals do best. Unfortunately, most humans are emotionally programmed to make bad choices when assessing risk. We follow the crowd, which causes us to buy at the top and sell at the bottom.

In my earlier discussion about real estate, in the example of how mortgage debt can help you in a disaster such as Katrina, our successful homeowner managed the risk of owning a home by investing his cash rather than paying down his mortgage. Wall Street lives and dies by statistical risk-reward ratios, extrapolated from past performance, in every tradable security.

In this supermarket of investment options, life insurance is a poor one. We pay now so someone else can get the reward after we're gone. But insurance offers a guarantee–an absence of risk–that's hard to beat. Insurance can play a major role in your financial planning.

BACK TO THE INSURANCE FUTURE

An insurance policy is essentially a contract in which only one party has to make a promise. The insured only has to pay the premiums. In our economy and in our laws, the inviolability of an insurance policy contract is well established. The insurance industry is highly-regulated, each insurance company is closely followed and rated for financial soundness, and the courts have tended to favor policy-holders in disputes.

For those and other reasons, insurance is a protective investment–for managing risk–and can play an important role in helping you hold on to the wealth you've saved and grown.

But there's insurance and then there's insurance. In the past several decades, the industry went through a transformation. Once dominated by mutual societies in which the policyholders also owned the company and by paying their premiums built cash value and earned dividends, today most insurance companies are publicly-held and beholden to shareholders. Policyholders are customers, the insurance contracts are products, and it's the goal of the broker or salesman to sell you the products that will earn him or her the largest commission, and the biggest profit for the company.

Today's insurance marketplace is rife with conflicts-of-interest, especially in variable annuities. Clients, let alone most agents, are unequipped to compare the hidden assumptions in different policies.

Today's insurance marketplace is rife with conflicts-of-interest, especially in variable annuities. Clients, let alone most agents, are unequipped to compare the hidden assumptions in different policies. Companies, through their agents, provide projections of what returns you might expect on any given product, but there are far too many variables to take such forecasts seriously. These figures have very little value in helping an investor choose what's right for them.

I encourage clients to ignore these projections because that's not the real value in insurance. It's all about the contract, the guarantees, the good faith and intentions of the company issuing the policy.

The ancient Greeks and Romans created the earliest known form of insurance when they organized guilds or benevolent societies that promised to pay final expenses of members and care for their families. We trace our current form of insurance to the 1600s when a London bar owner created the first market for managing risk in the maritime industry.

...during the Great Depression, while virtually all other asset classes were decimated, nobody lost money in their life insurance.

The first American life insurance enterprises were started in the late 1700s. By 1920 more than 300 life insurance companies were organized, most of them mutual societies owned by the policyholders. The industry's guiding principal was to protect their assets until the client needed them.

As a result, during the Great Depression, while virtually all other asset classes were decimated, nobody lost money in their life insurance. This gave the insurance industry a reputation for rock-solid trust and soundness.

Ever since the change began from mutual societies to stock-owned companies, the reputation of the insurance industry has eroded. Its lowest point so far came in the wake of Hurricane Katrina when an IPSOS-Public Affairs poll found that the only industry viewed less favorably by the public than insurance was oil and energy.

Once you've turned off all the marketing noise coming from today's insurance peddlers, the choice for those who want to protect their wealth is as stark as this: Would you rather own a life insurance contract backed by a 1,400-year-old tradition, or the latest marketing-driven insurance product aimed at boosting the earnings and meeting the shifting business needs of a company enslaved to the short-term demands of the stock market?

You won't hear it from an insurance salesman or broker, but you do hear it within the industry, out of earshot of consumers. Moody's Investor Services, which rates the financial soundness of insurance companies, pointed out in an April 2002 report that the mutual form of ownership "allows mutual companies to avoid the potential conflicts of interest that exist between policyholders and shareholders in publicly traded companies."

DIRECT RECOGNITION VS. NON-RECOGNITION CONTRACTS

Not all insurance was created equal. Some insurance contracts guarantee a fixed interest rate on loans–recognition contracts–and others provide for a variable rate–nonrecognition. All other things being equal, most people have an instinct to opt for a fixed-rate loan because they feel more secure knowing their cash flow needs. But the variable-rate contract is actually the better choice. The main difference between the two loan rates has more to do with the nature of the legal contract then the actual loan rate.

A recognition contract with a fixed-rate on loans you take out usually sets two different dividend levels. The dividend is the contractual promise that the company will distribute any excess profits above the amount retained to prudently run the business.

In a recognition contract, the company will pay one dividend rate for policies against which you have taken a loan and a higher dividend for policyholders who have not borrowed against their cash value.

In a recognition contract, the company will pay one dividend rate for policies against which you have taken a loan and a higher dividend for policyholders who have not borrowed against their cash value. This contract provides for a fixed loan rate, and gives the company more control over how profits are determined and distributed.

A non-recognition contract often has a variable interest rate with the cost of borrowing determined by an objective benchmark, such as the Moody's Corporate Bond Index Rate. Also, these type of contracts have the same dividend schedule as those who don't take out a loan.

The dividend on participating whole life comes from excess earnings on the cash left with the insurance company. This excess cash is usually invested in a conservative bond or corporate loan portfolio. Periodically, the excess earnings are classified as surplus earnings and are redistributed to the policy owner.

The non-recognition contract is the better choice in most circumstances because the excess earnings and the loan rate are pegged to the same objective source. The company has little or no control over how much of the profit is redirected to other corporate interests while non-recognition contracts give the policyholder, the owner, more control.

THE BASICS OF INSURANCE LOANS

Investors who contemplate borrowing against their policies are initially put off by the notion of paying interest for borrowing from themselves. But unlike a mortgage, where the interest payment belongs to the bank, the interest payment on an insurance loan, like the policy itself, belongs to you and is paid back to you.

A policyholder who borrows against the cash value of his or her policy has three options: don't pay it back, pay interest only, or pay principal and interest.

This is how each works:

...unlike a mortgage, where the interest payment belongs to the bank, the interest payment on an insurance loan, like the policy itself, belongs to you and is paid back to you.

Don't Pay It Back: This is the equivalent of withdrawing cash from your bank account–
you won't earn the dividend on the loan amount.

Pay Interest Only: The interest you pay will be added to your cash value.

Pay Principal and Interest: Both the principal and most, if not all, of the interest will be added to your cash value.

You choose how to treat this transaction, based on your particular financial plan and situation.

Participating whole life fits the criteria suggested by THE TEN TRUTHS OF WEALTH CREATION:

- The key to wealth is through ownership and control.

- Strive to minimize future decisions.

- Manage your tax obligations and recover lost opportunity costs such as interest income.

- Everything in life has a cost and requires payments.

16 A Brief Guide to Life Insurance

> What the insurance companies have done is to reverse the business so that the public at large insures the insurance companies.
> —Gerry Spencer, trial lawyer

LIFE INSURANCE CONTRACTS come in two basic forms: Term or Permanent. Term provides protection for a limited period or term. Whole life, Universal Life, or Variable life provide protection for one's entire life.

Term is similar to other types of insurance such as auto, homeowner's, and so on. You pay a premium for a specific coverage period and if no claim is made, you get nothing back.

Permanent insurance comes in a dizzying array of flavors–whole life participating, non-participating, universal, variable universal, variable, second-to-die, and modified endowment. These types of policies build equity as well as providing protection.

Term is the cheapest and most efficient way to cover a temporary planning need. If the need is lifelong–providing life insurance for heirs and other purposes when you die–participating whole life insurance is a better option for most, just as home ownership usually makes more sense than renting.

Life insurance is a unique asset. Because of its potential safe yield and its tax benefits, it can be used to solve some of life's perplexing financial problems.

Life insurance is a unique asset. Because of its potential safe yield and its tax benefits, it can be used to solve some of life's perplexing financial problems.

TYPICAL USES OF LIFE INSURANCE BENEFITS

Create an estate: When you've been unable to accumulate sufficient assets to care for heirs and loved ones, life insurance can create an instant estate.

Pay death taxes and estate costs: These costs can soak up more than half an estate's value.

Fund a business transfer: Business partners often agree that when one of them dies the other will buy their share from the estate. Life insurance provides the cash to finance the transaction.

Pay off a mortgage: To pass the family residence on free and clear, a decreasing-term policy is often used, with the face amount decreasing in synch with the pay-down of the mortgage.

Key person protection: Some businesses have employees who are essential to their operations and will buy policies that provide a benefit to the employer to get through the transition.

Replace a charitable gift: Gifts of appreciated assets to charitable remainder trusts can provide income and estate tax benefits while you are living, and the value for heirs can be offset by life insurance. Proceeds from life insurance policies can also be paid directly to a charity.

Pay off loans: Outstanding personal or business loans can be paid off with insurance proceeds.

Equalize inheritances: When a family business is part of the estate and there are children who are active in it, life insurance provides a way of sharing the inheritance without having to refinance the business.

Accelerated death benefits: The Health Insurance Portability and Accountability Act of 1996 changed federal tax law to allow a terminally-ill person to receive the death benefits of a life insurance policy while they are living, in some cases free of income tax. This provides funds to pay medical bills or other care expenses.

College fund: Increases in cash value of whole life contracts–on the student's life or the parent's–can help fund college expenses.

Supplement retirement funds: Current insurance products provide competitive returns and are a prudent way of accumulating additional funds for retirement.

TYPES OF LIFE INSURANCE POLICIES

Different types of policies serve different needs:

Decreasing Term:
Premium doesn't change, coverage gradually decreases, and has no cash value. Often used to match financial obligations that shrink with time, such as a mortgage or other amortized loan.

Annual Renewable Term: Premium increases over time, coverage stays the same, has no cash value. Often chosen for financial obligations which remain constant for a short or intermediate period, such as income during a minor's dependency. This type has the lowest cost to begin, but it increases each year.

Long Term, Level Premium: Premium and coverage stay the same, has no cash value. Annual premiums are fixed for the term, typically five, ten, fifteen, or twenty years. Least expensive way to cover a large temporary need.

Whole Life: Level premium, level coverage, builds cash value. Cash value increases based on insurance company's portfolio performance. These policies come in both participating and non-participating.

Universal Life: Level or adjustable premium and coverage, builds cash value. Cash values may increase, based on the performance of certain assets held in the company's general account.

Variable/Variable Universal Life: Level/adjustable premium, level coverage, cash value. Same as universal life or non-participating whole life, but the insured has better control of the outcome because they can invest the portion of the premium not used for term insurance in investments tied to the stock and bond markets.

Single Premium Whole Life: Entire premium is paid in advance, cash value, level coverage: Provides protection as well as serving as an asset accumulation vehicle.

TERM LIFE INSURANCE

Types of term insurance include:

Annual renewable term: Level death benefit, premium increases each year, no cash value.

Long-term level, premium term: Premiums are fixed for specified period of time, typically five, ten, fifteen, or twenty years. Death benefit remains constant, no cash value.

Decreasing Term: Premium stays the same, death benefit decreases over time, no cash value.

Combination policies: Term life insurance is sometimes teamed with a permanent policy to provide the benefits of both types. In the family income policy and family maintenance policy, for example, a term policy with a decreasing death benefit is combined with a permanent, level benefit policy.

COMMON USES OF TERM INSURANCE

Term life insurance is most useful when an insured is younger and needs temporary or short-term coverage. Some common uses of term insurance include:

Family protection: To provide funds to support a surviving spouse and/or minor children, and to pay final medical and/or estate expenses.

Declining needs: Sometimes a debt, such as a mortgage, is matched with a decreasing term policy. As the debt is paid off, the policy's death benefit is reduced.

Business planning: A business may use term insurance to insure a key employee, or to recruit or retain key employees through a salary continuation plan.

For business partners, insurance is also useful as a way to fund a cross-purchase, buy-sell agreement, particularly when one owner is significantly younger than another.

Charitable gifts: To provide funds for a gift to charity.

Optional policy provisions: Riders–optional provisions–can be added to a basic term life policy, through payment of an additional premium.

Renewable: Allows policy to be renewed at the end of the term without the insured having to show that he or she is still insurable.

Convertible: Provides the option to convert a term policy to a permanent policy, usually without having to prove good health.

Accidental death: Pays double or more if insured dies in an accident. The kind of insurance Barbara Stanwyck was trying to collect on in the 1944 murder thriller, "Double Indemnity."

Waiver of premium:
Allows an insured to stop paying premiums if he or she becomes disabled and is unable to work.

Accelerated death benefits: Allows partial benefit payment while an insured is still alive, typically when the insured is considered to be terminally ill.

WHOLE LIFE INSURANCE

Whole life insurance is often referred to as ordinary or permanent life. These policies are designed to stay in force throughout one's lifetime.

These policies are designed to stay in force throughout one's lifetime.

Unlike term insurance, where premiums generally increase with age as the chance of death increases, whole life premiums remain constant. Over time, a whole life policy's cash value increases. Most clients considering a whole life contract are concerned about the lack of return in the first year. But compared with a like investment in a home, if you sold the home in the first year, chances are that the transaction costs and transfer taxes would eat up any gain benefit. So when comparing the two, the outcome is essentially the same.

Many whole life policies allow you to borrow a portion of the accumulated cash value. If a policy is terminated while the insured is living, there are various surrender options for the policy owner to get the cash value.

WHOLE LIFE POLICY VARIATIONS

There are two primary types of whole life insurance, based on the period over which the premium payments are made.

Ordinary life: An ordinary life policy assumes that premiums will be paid until the insured dies. Premiums are based on the assumption that the insured will die by a certain age, typically age 100. If an insured lives to this age, the policy pays the face amount of the death benefit.

Limited-payment life: This type assumes that all premium payments are made over a specified, limited period, typically ranging from one to thirty years. Premiums for a limited-payment life policy are generally higher than for an ordinary life policy, because the payment period is shorter.

ADDITIONAL WHOLE LIFE POLICY ELEMENTS

Whole life policies often have additional, useful features:

Policy loans: Almost all whole life policies permit the policy owner to borrow a portion of the accumulated cash value, with the insurance company charging interest on the loan. The rate charged is often lower than competitive market rates. A policy loan will reduce the death benefit payable if the insured dies before the loan and any interest due is repaid. A policy loan will also reduce the cash surrender value if a policy is terminated. If a policy lapses or is surrendered with a loan outstanding, the loan will be treated as taxable income for the current year, to the extent of gain in the policy.

Policy dividends: Whole life contracts classified as "participating" offer the possibility of policy "dividends," which are not guaranteed but represent a return to the policy owner of part of the premium paid. A dividend may be taken as cash or a policy may offer a number of other ways the dividend might be used:

• To reduce current premium payments

- To buy additional, paid-up insurance, known as paid-up additions
- To be retained by the insurer, earning interest for the policyholder
- To purchase one-year term insurance
- To be added to the policy's cash value
- To pay up the policy earlier than scheduled

OPTIONAL POLICY PROVISIONS-RIDERS

A number of optional provisions called riders can be added to a basic whole life policy and all permanent contracts through payment of an additional premium:

Waiver of premium: Allows an insured to stop paying premiums if he or she becomes disabled or is unable to work.

Accidental death: Pays the beneficiaries double or triple the benefit if the insured dies in an accident.

Spousal or family term insurance: Allows a policy owner to purchase term insurance on a spouse or children.

Accelerated death benefits: Allows payment of part of a policy's death benefit while an insured is still alive. Such benefits are typically payable when the insured develops a medical condition expected to lead to death within a short period of time.

UNIVERSAL LIFE INSURANCE

Universal life differs from traditional whole life by specifically separating and identifying the mortality, expense, and cash value parts of a policy. This allows more flexibility to modify the policy face amount or premium, in response to changing needs or circumstances.

The problem with these new type of contracts–offered by stock-owned insurance companies–is that a lower return on the cash value has a corresponding increasing cost on the term insurance component. Many consumers in the late 1970s and 1980s

Many consumers in the late 1970s and 1980s replaced perfectly sound whole life contracts with universal life since the illustrations showed that then-prevailing high returns could substantially reduce premium payments.

replaced perfectly sound whole life contracts with universal life since the illustrations showed that then-prevailing high returns could substantially reduce premium payments. As rates fell, many who purchased these contracts have had to double and triple premium payments to keep their policies in force.

POLICY VARIATIONS

There are two primary types of universal life, based on the level of death benefits.

Type I (option "A") universal life: Pays a fixed death benefit. The cost decreases as the cash value increases.

Type II (option "B") universal life: Pays a fixed death benefit plus the accumulated cash value. As the cash value grows, so does the death benefit.

VARIABLE LIFE INSURANCE

Variable life insurance, like whole life, features fixed premiums, and a minimum guaranteed death benefit. However, variable life permits the policy owner to allocate a portion of each premium payment to one or more investment options, after certain deductions.

The death benefit and cash value of a variable life policy will increase or decrease based on the performance of the investment options chosen. The death benefit, however, will not drop below an initial guaranteed amount, assuming premiums are paid and no loans or other withdrawals are taken.

Because the investment options usually involve stocks and bonds, the Securities and Exchange Commission (SEC) requires this type of policy to be accompanied by a prospectus. The prospectus provides detailed information on how the policy works, its risks, and all expenses or charges. The SEC also requires individuals selling variable life policies to be licensed to sell securities.

POLICY VARIATIONS

There are two primary variations on variable life insurance, based on the formula used to link the amount of death benefit to the performance of the investments. In general, if the investment has grown, the amount of the death benefit increases. If investment performance is negative, the death benefit amount will decrease.

Corridor percentage: Also know as the constant ratio method, the amount of the death benefit is linked to the cash value. Under current tax law, this percentage is 250 percent up to the insured's fortieth birthday, then gradually decreasing to 100 percent, usually at age ninety-five.

Level additions: Also known as the net single premium approach, this method uses excess investment earnings to purchase additional single premium, paid-up insurance.

COMMON USES OF VARIABLE LIFE

Variable life policies are well suited for use by policy owners who are comfortable with the risks and rewards of investments, and who need life insurance with the potential to provide an increasing death benefit. One potential problem with variable life is that the death benefit is affected by the performance of the investments.

ADDITIONAL POLICY ELEMENTS

Most variable life policies offer a wide range of investment options, including basic stock, bond, and money market funds. Depending on the policy and insurer, other options may include index funds, real estate funds, foreign stock funds, or zero coupon bond funds. A policy may also include a fixed account option, in which the insurer guarantees a fixed rate of return backed by a general asset pool.

Variable life policies classified as participating offer the possibility of policy dividends. Dividends from a participating variable life policy are not guaranteed, and represent a return to the policy owner of a portion of the premium paid. Most participating policies offer a number of options as to how the dividends may be used.

VARIABLE UNIVERSAL LIFE INSURANCE

A variable universal life insurance policy combines features in both universal and variable policies.

Since the cost is related to investment returns, there is either a positive or negative compounding effect. However, most variable life insurance proposals assume a consistent compounded market return of about 10 percent. As we showed earlier, you can have an average return of 10 percent and actually end up with an actual return of zero. These assumptions are useless in financial planning because the markets have never returned 10 percent every year and in any year that has a negative return, not only will the cash value shrink, the shrinkage will be exacerbated by an increasing cost of the term insurance element.

MODIFIED ENDOWMENT CONTRACTS (MECS)

A life insurance policy issued on or after June 21, 1988 may be classified as a modified endowment contract (MEC) if the cumulative premiums paid during the first seven years exceed the total of the net level premiums for the same period. If one invests too much money, the policy will lose its favorable tax benefits.

If a policy is classified as a MEC, all withdrawals, including loans, will be taxed as current income until all of the policy earnings have been taxed. There is an additional 10 percent penalty tax if the owner is under age fifty-nine and a-half at the time of withdrawal, unless the payments are due to disability or are annuity type payments.

FIRST-TO-DIE OR SECOND-TO-DIE LIFE INSURANCE POLICIES

First-to-die and second-to-die, also known as joint-life insurance policies, pay out the face amount when the first or second named insured dies. This reduces the cost of paying premiums on two separate policies, when the insurance proceeds are most needed when only the first or second insured dies. The following examples illustrate how this type of policy can be effectively used.

BUY-SELL FUNDING

A corporation or partnership with two or more owners often experiences problems in transferring ownership to a surviving owner or owners and paying a fair cash price to the deceased owner's heirs. This problem is usually remedied with a properly structured buy-sell agreement, which assures a fair price for the decedent's share of the business and allows the surviving business partner to retain control and ownership of the business.

Life insurance is well established as the ideal method of funding buy-sell agreements. By using a joint-life policy, the company may be able to reduce the amount of cash flow required to pay the premiums, while still guaranteeing that the funds will be available for the buy-out no matter which partner or shareholder dies first.

KEY PERSON PROTECTION

The loss of a key employee or executive can have a devastating effect on a business. The use of joint-life policies can reduce the required cash flow to insure against the loss of any one person from a selected group of key persons. Insurance proceeds can be used to find, recruit, and train replacement employees and sustain or strengthen the company's credit position.

WORKING COUPLES

With many families relying on two incomes, it is prudent to insure against the loss of either spouse. The joint-life policy should be considered as part of the solution to the loss of income from the death of either spouse.

ESTATE FUNDING OF AN IRREVOCABLE INSURANCE TRUST

The second-to–die contract is the most common contract for funding an irrevocable trust. The main purpose is to provide funds for a family to pay estate taxes which are typically owed on the second death. This enables the beneficiaries to inherit the greater portion of an estate while avoiding being forced to liquidate assets or real estate to pay the death taxes.

17 The Life Insurance Purchase You Never See

Consistently wise decisions can only be made by those whose wisdom is constantly challenged.
—Theodore C. Sorensen, Presidential historian

ALTHOUGH OLD-FASHIONED defined benefit pensions are being replaced by plans like 401(k)s, many employees–especially civil service–are still protected by these old plans and the decisions they make on how to draw their benefits can cost heirs millions. Understanding the components will enable you to make an educated, instead of emotional, decision.

Most defined benefit pensions pay a percentage of salary at retirement. In most cases, retirees receive an annuity income for the rest of their lives, or for the combined lives of themselves and a spouse. The choice most married people tend to make is the "I-love-you" option that guarantees an income for both partners. But what seems to make the most sense can actually end up robbing your spouse of substantial financial security.

For illustration purposes, assume that an employee has earned a benefit at retirement age of sixty-five of $35,000 a

year, which will cease upon his or her death. If the pensioner chooses instead to opt for the "I-love-you" option–known as Joint and Full Survivor–the annual payment is reduced to about $29,000 for the lifetimes of both spouses. (There are many variations on this, such as joint and two-thirds survivor, or joint and 50 percent survivor.)

Most people calculate that the lower income is worth the guarantee that the surviving spouse will receive an income to their last day. But few people realize that by doing so, they will have purchased a very expensive life insurance policy. It is a policy that you cannot change, has no cash value, and no living benefits.

Between the roughly $6,000 a year that will have been given up to guarantee the spouse an income ($29,000 instead of $35,000), plus any cost of living increase built into the pension, over twenty years more than $250,000 will have been lost.

If your spouse happens to die first, you will have given up this additional income for your life without anyone receiving a benefit upon your death. And what if both spouses die soon after retirement? There's nothing left for the heirs.

Furthermore, the pension payments are taxed as ordinary income, which could mean a tax bite of as much as 35 percent, leaving only about $19,000 in actual survivor income.

THE SOLUTION

The pensioner can avoid this lost opportunity by electing to take the higher benefit of $35,000 if, through careful planning, the pensioner has a life insurance policy that provides a tax-free death benefit to guarantee that their family will receive the equivalent of their pension in a lump sum.

In a normal pension, joint and survivor payments stop on the death of the second spouse. If the spouse dies first or at the same time, the value of the life insurance passes on to the next of kin.

In a normal pension, joint and survivor payments stop on the death of the second spouse. If the spouse dies first or at the same time, the value of the life insurance passes on to the next of kin.

In addition to providing the family with potentially more income in retirement, the death benefit can be tapped to provide long term care for the insured. If both spouses live long enough, they will have the cash value in their insurance plan to tap to improve their lifestyle.

As in any financial decision, there are numerous factors to consider, such as the health of the retiree at retirement.

People too often make important decisions on the fly without analyzing the details, then building a solution that could provide more flexibility and much greater financial security.

18 Life Insurance FAQs

AT SEMINARS I LEAD on wealth creation, few topics bewilder people more than life insurance, especially the "living benefits." They are just as important, and often more so, than the death benefits.

I have discussed using life insurance as a safe place to park cash instead of in a bank. Additional benefits include:

- Disability savings
- Long term care protection
- Enhancing income
- Liability and bankruptcy protection
- Tax-free growth
- Tax-free death benefits
- A bank account to recapture costs of living
- Recapturing lost opportunity costs from paying taxes

To explain some of these living benefits, here are some questions I'm frequently asked about how life insurance works:

INSURANCE AS DISABILITY PROTECTION

Q. I have disability insurance at work. How can life insurance provide me with disability protection?

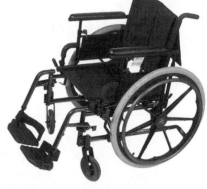

A. Most disability plans pay some income if you become permanently disabled, about 60 percent to age sixty-five. If your financial plan projections include pension contributions from you and your employer, as well as savings into a college savings plan, all bets are off when you become disabled.

Your employer will no longer be making pension or Social Security contributions. At 60 percent of your salary, it will become much more difficult, if not impossible, to save for college. Disability income does not replace savings and you may need to find another way to live after age sixty-five.

Solution: If you were saving into a life insurance policy, you can add a "waiver of premium benefit" on your contract, so that if you became disabled, the insurance company would pay the premium for the rest of your life, guaranteeing that at least a portion of your savings will continue.

INSURANCE AND FLEXIBILITY

Q. Does it make sense to tie up my investment with one insurance company for 30 years?

A. I'm not arguing that life insurance is the best place to put your dollars forever. But it is a good place to start building the foundation of your financial future. In the late 1970s, plain vanilla, ultra-safe money market accounts paid up to 18 percent. Long-term bonds in a portfolio managed inside an insurance contract paid 6 percent. Policy holders called up their insurance companies complaining and were told they could either surrender the contract or borrow the cash value. Most surrendered the contract but they could have borrowed their cash at 6 percent, reinvested it in a money market paying 18 percent but only pay taxes on the difference of 12 percent. This arrangement becomes even sweeter when you consider that most, if not all, of the interest you pay on your cash value loan goes back into your account.

INSURANCE AS INVESTMENT

Q. Will I earn more money investing in the stock market or real estate?

A. To invest in anything, you first have to accumulate the cash. Using an insurance contract to save–to accumulate your cash–may take slightly longer but it provides a guarantee of the outcome. All investments we purchase–stocks, bonds or real estate–incur a tax liability. Although insurance contracts come with a cost, it never exceeds tax cost over time and you receive benefits in your lifetime and beyond.

ADVANTAGES OF WHOLE LIFE OVER VARIABLE LIFE

Q. If one is a risk-taker, why not just purchase a variable life contract instead of a participating whole life contract?

A. Variable insurance typically offers a fixed account offered through a stock company with lower yields. With whole life, by using the loan provision, you can deduct the interest expense from your investment earnings and invest in anything in the marketplace, such as bank CDs, bonds, stocks, exchange-traded funds, real estate, or even a personal business. Why put your dollars in an investment in which your options are limited?

INSURANCE AS INCOME ENHANCEMENT

Q. How does having life insurance enhance ones income?

A. A retiree's greatest worry is running out of money, or not leaving enough for their dependents. Investment advisors and accountants often counsel clients to draw minimum distributions from their retirement account or IRA, to avoid touching principal.

Suppose one has $500,000 in an IRA and their total tax rate is 30 percent. That means they only have $350,000 to work with. If they want to live on the interest, assuming a 6 percent return, they will only receive $30,000 a year, or $21,000.00 in spendable dollars.

If, instead, they had a $350,000 life insurance policy they used as their bank account, they could spend down their IRA over their lifetime and still have assets for long term care or inheritance. Between ages sixty-five and eighty-eight, that would enable them to increase their income for living to about $38,000, far more than the insurance policy cost.

INSURANCE FOR LONG TERM CARE

Q. How does life insurance protect me in the case of long-term care?

A. Life insurance contracts today are often available with both an accelerated death benefit and a long-term care rider. These riders enable someone to use not just the cash value but the death benefit to meet long term care expenses. To purchase insurance just for long-term care is to lock up your money for a very limited purpose and use. One can pay premiums on a long-term care contract for thirty years and then suddenly die of a heart attack and get no benefit at all. Life insurance with a long-term care provision guarantees a return one way or the other.

INSURANCE OPTIONS FOR THE TERMINALLY ILL

The stress of a terminal illness is compounded by medical bills and loss of income. A person owning life insurance policies may have several options for reducing some of these financial concerns.

Borrow against cash values: Whole life, variable life, universal life, and other types of permanent insurance build up cash values over the years that can be borrowed against, often at favorable interest rates. Upon death, the policy loans and any interest will be subtracted from the face amount before payment is made to the beneficiary. If there is also a "waiver of premium" provision, the insured may be relieved of the monthly premium payments, under certain circumstances.

Surrender the policy: Policies with accumulated cash values can be surrendered to the life insurance company. However this is generally undesirable since the face amount of the policy is usually much higher than the surrender value. If death is imminent, this could be a very costly option for beneficiaries.

Borrow funds from a third party: Friends, family, and possibly the beneficiary of the policy may be willing to lend money to the person who is terminally ill, and receive repayment from the insurance proceeds.

Accelerated death benefits: Some life policies provide for payment of a portion of the face amount if the insured becomes terminally ill. This is generally called a "living benefit" or an "accelerated death benefit." Even if it is not mentioned in the policy, the company may extend the right to the policy owner if death is anticipated within six to nine months.

Another option is to sell one's life policy to a third party in exchange for a percentage of the face amount. This is called a viatical settlement, derived from the Latin word "viaticum," which means "supplies for a difficult journey." These settlements may also be available with contracts that have no cash value such as individual or group term life insurance policies. Factors which will determine the amount of the settlement include the insured's life expectancy. The shorter the period, the more a viatical settlement the company will pay. Some companies will pay on up to a five-year life expectancy, but many prefer a shorter term. Viatical settlement companies generally offer between 25 percent and 85 percent of the policy's face amount.

The sale of one's life insurance policies can have far reaching consequences and should be done only after consulting an attorney, certified public accountant, or other professional advisors.

Terminally ill persons who have been diagnosed by a physician as likely to die within twenty-four months may receive accelerated death benefits free of federal income taxes. Chronically ill individuals may also exclude from taxes income-accelerated death benefits which are used to pay the actual costs of qualified long-term care.

INSURANCE AS LIABILITY/BANKRUPTCY PROTECTION

Q. How does owning a life insurance contract protect me in a lawsuit or bankruptcy?

A. Many state laws protect the cash value of a life insurance contract from liability in law suits and bankruptcy because the benefit is for someone else. Some states allow you to pay back insurance loans before a court can attach any of your assets in liability or bankruptcy settlements. Insurance can be a safe place to protect your wealth.

THE WELL-KEPT SECRET OF INSURANCE

Q. Why doesn't everyone use insurance the way you've explained?

A. These concepts are used by some of America's largest corporations, like Disney, Dow Chemical, and Wal-Mart, to name a few. Companies use life insurance contracts to park their cash and then borrow the cash value to fund operations. In corporate finance circles, these contracts are commonly referred to as "janitorial policies." A company will buy an insurance contract on all employees, then borrow the cash value and deduct the interest expense against earnings. The IRS has begun to investigate these contract abuses since there is little or no insurable interest. But the fact that smart accountants for big companies have figured out what a great deal this is should tell you that, for your legitimate purposes, it's a useful tool in financial planning.

As in most aspects of life, what counts is not how we start but how we end up. In financial planning, one must start by building a strong foundation, and then all other opportunities become available. Life insurance is the only product that provides this foundation throughout one's lifetime.

PART VI

Integrating the Parts

19 Taxes Are An After-Tax Payment

> Can taxation without representation
> be any worse than it is with it?
> —Sydney J. Harris, syndicated newspaper columnist

FOR THE VAST MAJORITY OF US, the money we spend to buy just about anything has been taxed at least once, and often many times. Culturally, we tend to have a fatalistic attitude about taxes–just a cost of living. But there are hidden costs that we ignore at our expense.

For example, Social Security and Medicare taxes take 7.65 percent of your gross income before income taxes. In order to pay Social Security and Medicare taxes of $1,000, assuming you're in the 35 percent bracket, you have to earn $1,539.49 in pre-tax income. So your Social Security and Medicare taxes are an after-tax payment.

Taxes have many important and manageable effects on your financial planning. For example, financial planners have a tendency to overstate the need for income in retirement. If a couple pays $8,000 a year in Social Security taxes before retirement, most financial planners will reduce their financial needs by that $8,000, since social security taxes are not taken out of retirement income.

Taxes have many important and manageable effects on your financial planning. For example, financial planners have a tendency to overstate the need for income in retirement.

But, the actual cost to pay $8,000 a year in Social Security taxes is about $12,300, assuming a 35 percent tax bite. Over the course of a thirty-year retirement period, the over-estimate of income needs is about $130,000.

It's no wonder that planning for our financial future causes so much stress that people tend to avoid it.

Two areas of the tax code that have remained inviolate over the decades are the federal deductibility of state income taxes and real estate or property taxes. Our government uses the latter to promote ownership of property which helps the economy grow.

State income taxes remain deductible because more tax revenue would go to the federal government and it would be harder for the states to raise money.

THE COMPOUND TAX PROBLEM

The combination of income taxes, lost opportunity costs on the income taxes, inflation, and estate taxes can erase a lot of your investment gains.

Compounding is a powerful engine for growing money but compounding also drives taxes and inflation. As you accumulate money, time gradually erodes its buying power. As a result, the miracle of compound interest can cost consumers more money than it makes, especially in taxable savings and investments. The combination of income taxes, lost opportunity costs on the income taxes, inflation, and estate taxes can erase a lot of your investment gains.

For example, a $50,000 investment earning 6 percent interest for thirty years will yield almost $290,000. Income taxes in a 40 percent marginal tax bracket will come to about $95,000. Inflation for thirty years at 3 percent takes away buying power of nearly $170,000.

So the cost of growing $50,000 to $290,000 over thirty years is about $315,000.

But it's actually worse than that. The income taxes were paid out-of-pocket. So, there's also a lost opportunity on what those tax payments could have been worth in thirty years had they been saved or invested. And if you die with the account in your estate, it may be subject to inheritance taxes.

It is crucial in financial planning to assess the amount of time your money will compound, and consider the hidden costs of taxation and inflation.

TAXES AND MYTHS

There is a well-used example in the investment discussion that you may have run across. Mary opens at IRA when she is eighteen years old and puts in $2000 a year for four years in an 8 percent investment. Then she marries, stops working, and never contributes another nickel. She retires at the age of sixty-five and her investment of $8,000 had grown to about $285,000.

John doesn't settle down until he's thirty-five, when he begins to put $2,000 a year into an IRA, and continues to do so for 30 years, contributing a total of $62,000. He retires at 65 with about $265,000, roughly $20,000 less than Mary.

This is a terrific example of how compounding works, but something's been left out. John, at age thirty-five, was in a 35 percent tax bracket so he saved about $19,000 more in taxes. One variable alters the results.

A PERSONAL EXAMPLE OF WEALTH LOST

After thirty years working for Proctor Silex, a manufacturer of household appliances, my grandfather retired at age sixty-five with a gold watch and the house he bought in 1956 for $6,000. He owned some stock in a utility company and had received regular dividend checks for decades. Over the years, my grandparents let their dividends be reinvested and watched their little fortune grow.

After my grandfather had died, and my grandmother reached ninety-one years of age, utility stocks declined due to aging plants and other economic considerations. The utility shares were worth about $40,000 and I was concerned that, with years and years of dividends being reinvested, if we sold the stock how would we ever be able to determine the cost basis for tax purposes.

We contacted the utility company to get a basis for the stock my grandparents had accumulated bit by bit during forty years. When we finally got the numbers, I was shocked to discover that not only would there be no tax bill to pay, but my grandparents had an actual loss of $13,000. My grandfather had paid taxes on approximately $53,000 in dividend income to accumulate stock worth $40,000.

That sad result doesn't even take into account lost opportunity costs, and lost income potential on the taxes he paid. This is how wealth is squandered.

THE COMPOUND TAX, LOST OPPORTUNITY COST CONVERSATION

When analyzing investment opportunities, it is usually risk, return, and impact of taxes that receive the closest evaluation. But to limit the evaluation to those factors alone overlooks the longer-term effect that the compounding of tax payments can have over the total life of an investment.

The criteria that I encourage clients to consider include:

> *Lost opportunity cost is that part of your investment that stops working for you, and the earnings potential that the loss represents.*

Investment Vehicle:
Is the assumed rate of return appropriate for the anticipated investment period?

Return Calculation:
Are the returns computed on a simple or compounded basis, and are the returns on CDs, bank accounts, and daily-market based investments net or gross of fees?

Taxes Paid: Are you applying an average, marginal, or graduated tax bracket, and have you considered all Federal, State, and County taxes?

Lost Opportunity Costs: What will be the reduction to the portfolio from taxes paid and the potential earnings lost on taxes paid?

Income Reinvestment: What is the effect of reinvested interest, dividends and/or capital gains.

EXAMPLE: HOW LIFE INSURANCE CAN RECOVER LOST OPPORTUNITY COSTS

Even if you have your money in a taxed investment, rather than rolling over the income and letting the principal accumulate, you can reinvest the income by paying premiums on a participating whole life policy where the dividends are untaxed. In the chart below you can see how, instead of paying taxes on income that's already been taxed (See chart on page 85), you can save yourself almost $160,000 over 30 years.

$100,000 AT 6% RETURN FOR 30 YEARS
WITH AFTER-TAX INCOME INVESTED IN LIFE INSURANCE

	Beginning of Year Value	Assumed Earnings for the Year	Less Transfers to Tax-Free Alternative	Year End Value (Before Taxes)	Life-to-Date Taxes Paid Out-of-Pocket	Earnings Compounded on Taxes Paid Out-of-Pocket:	Cummulative Taxes & Lost Opportunity Cost:	Lost Opportunity Cost Recovered
1st year:	100,000	6,000	(6,000)	100,000	1,800	108	1,908	0
2nd year:	100,000	6,000	(6,000)	100,000	3,600	330	3,930	114
3rd year:	100,000	6,000	(6,000)	100,000	5,400	674	6,074	357
4th year:	100,000	6,000	(6,000)	100,000	7,200	1,147	8,347	743
5th year:	100,000	6,000	(6,000)	100,000	9,000	1,756	10,756	1,288
10th year:	100,000	6,000	(6,000)	100,000	18,000	7,149	25,149	7,086
15th year:	100,000	6,000	(6,000)	100,000	27,000	17,411	44,411	20,297
20th year:	100,000	6,000	(6,000)	100,000	36,000	34,187	70,187	45,270
25th year:	100,000	6,000	(6,000)	100,000	45,000	59,681	104,681	88,453
30th year:	100,000	6,000	(6,000)	100,000	54,000	96,843	150,843	159,306

A 6% annual return in a tax-free investment | Opportunity Cost Recovered

Running the numbers:
Assuming $100,000 invested at 6% taxable, for 25 years

Tax free, you'd end up with..........................$429,187
Paying taxes, reinvesting income
     in same taxable investment...............$236,053
LOST OPPORTUNITY COST...............................$193,134

THE SOLUTION: Invest all after-tax income in participating whole life policy with dividends tax free

Recovered lost opportunity cost.........$ 88,453
Policy guaranteed cash value...........+$175,141
MINIMUM TOTAL WEALTH CREATED...............$258,912
PROJECTED WEALTH (per div. history)............$360,456

THE LIFE INSURANCE BONUS: The life insurance choice also gives you death, long-term care, and disability benefits.

A Hypothetical Life Insurance Illustration
Assuming policyholder is male, age 40, preferred

		Guaranteed			Non-Guaranteed Assumptions 100% of Current Dividend Scale					
Age	Year	Contract Premium	Net Cash Value	Death Benefit	Contract Premium	Cum Premium	Annual Dividend	Increase in Net Cash Value	Net Cash Value	Death Benefit
41	1	6,000	2,931	178,717	6,000	6,000	107	3,037	3,037	179,200
42	2	6,000	5,975	191,479	6,000	12,000	272	3,320	6,358	193,144
43	3	6,000	10,720	203,761	6,000	18,000	443	5,203	11,561	207,283
44	4	6,000	15,978	215,583	6,000	24,000	634	5,924	17,484	221,665
45	5	6,000	21,416	226,967	6,000	30,000	832	6,328	23,813	236,286
46	6	6,000	27,167	237,933	6,000	36,000	1,049	6,890	30,703	251,181
47	7	6,000	33,116	248,498	6,000	42,000	1,279	7,360	38,063	266,364
48	8	6,000	39,276	258,682	6,000	48,000	1,508	7,853	45,916	281,795
49	9	6,000	45,669	268,498	6,000	54,000	1,745	8,386	54,302	297,466
50	10	6,000	52,294	277,960	6,000	60,000	1,994	8,942	63,244	313,379
51	11	6,000	59,155	287,082	6,000	66,000	2,244	9,512	72,756	329,498
52	12	6,000	66,239	295,877	6,000	72,000	2,533	10,118	82,874	345,912
53	13	6,000	73,544	304,359	6,000	78,000	2,842	10,756	93,630	362,641
54	14	6,000	81,066	312,542	6,000	84,000	3,173	11,421	105,050	379,712
55	15	6,000	88,788	320,439	6,000	90,000	3,509	12,083	117,133	397,101
56	16	6,000	96,707	328,066	6,000	96,000	3,836	12,746	129,879	414,753
57	17	6,000	104,825	335,436	6,000	102,000	4,184	13,443	143,322	432,693
58	18	6,000	113,164	342,560	6,000	108,000	4,491	14,138	157,460	450,792
59	19	6,000	121,737	349,451	6,000	114,000	4,812	14,874	172,334	469,056
60	20	6,000	130,537	356,117	6,000	120,000	5,165	15,647	187,981	487,539
61	21	6,000	139,179	362,569	6,000	126,000	5,557	16,077	204,057	506,303
62	22	6,000	147,978	368,816	6,000	132,000	6,004	16,881	220,938	525,439
63	23	6,000	156,908	374,870	6,000	138,000	6,495	17,705	238,643	545,013
64	24	6,000	165,961	380,740	6,000	144,000	7,023	18,566	257,210	565,070
65	25	6,000	175,141	386,437	6,000	150,000	7,579	19,475	276,685	585,633
66	26	5,892	184,454	391,969	5,892	155,892	8,154	20,427	297,112	606,707
67	27	5,892	193,921	397,344	5,892	161,785	8,749	21,444	318,556	628,295
68	28	5,892	203,549	402,569	5,892	167,677	9,368	22,508	341,064	650,403
69	29	5,892	213,354	407,652	5,892	173,570	10,011	23,640	364,704	673,039
70	30	5,892	223,318	412,596	5,892	179,462	10,706	24,812	389,516	696,256
71	31	5,892	233,416	417,409	5,892	185,354	11,463	26,026	415,543	720,122
72	32	5,892	243,591	422,096	5,892	191,247	12,320	27,260	442,802	744,763
73	33	5,892	253,795	426,664	5,892	197,139	13,268	28,522	471,324	770,290
74	34	5,892	264,038	431,119	5,892	203,032	14,245	29,842	501,166	796,706
75	35	5,892	274,328	435,466	5,892	208,924	15,269	31,241	532,406	824,044
76	36	5,892	284,658	439,712	5,892	214,817	16,341	32,686	565,092	852,333
77	37	5,892	295,002	443,862	5,892	220,709	17,496	34,182	599,274	881,656
78	38	5,892	305,309	447,919	5,892	226,601	18,759	35,707	634,981	912,129
79	39	5,892	315,519	451,890	5,892	232,494	20,143	37,247	672,228	943,882
80	40	5,892	325,592	455,779	5,892	238,386	21,632	38,814	711,042	977,024
81	41	5,892	335,494	459,593	5,892	244,279	23,220	40,414	451,456	1,011,655
82	42	5,892	345,213	463,336	5,892	250,171	24,885	42,068	793,524	1,047,842
83	43	5,892	354,772	467,012	5,892	256,064	26,576	43,791	837,316	1,085,587
84	44	5,892	364,154	470,627	5,892	261,956	28,353	45,554	882,870	1,124,968
85	45	5,892	373,331	474,185	5,892	267,849	30,243	47,364	930,234	1,166,101
86	46	5,892	382,258	477,688	5,892	273,741	32,254	49,172	979,406	1,209,112
87	47	5,892	390,892	481,142	5,892	279,633	34,383	50,968	1,030,374	1,254,127
88	48	5,892	399,220	484,551	5,892	285,526	36,625	52,815	1,083,189	1,301,269
89	49	5,892	407,234	487,918	5,892	291,418	38,957	54,672	1,137,861	1,350,636
90	50	5,892	414,945	491,248	5,892	297,311	41,355	56,564	1,194,424	1,402,302

20 Discipline & Single-Decision Solutions

> *A journey of a thousand miles must begin with the first step.*
> —Lao Tzu, ancient Chinese philosopher

IN FINANCIAL PLAN-NING SEMINARS I have been invited to give at company sites, there are those who bring their lunch to work and others who run out to the local delicatessen to buy a sandwich, bag of chips, and a soda. I would begin the sessions by pointing to the brown-baggers and explaining to the others that the decision to buy their lunch could be costing them over a million dollars during their lifetimes.

The reaction is always skeptical, but then I crunch the numbers.

AFTER-TAX RETURN OF BROWN BAGGING YOUR LUNCH

- If you spend $10 a day on convenience foods (sandwiches, sodas, snacks, coffee), four days per week, you are spending about $2,000 a year more than if you brown-bagged it.

- If, instead, you invested $2,000 a year at 6%, at the end of 20 years you'd have more than $80,000 saved. At the end of 30 years, you'd have about $175,000, and after 40 years, it would come to about $340,000.

- If you had invested the $2,000 and managed to get a return of 10%, at the end of 40 years you'd have about $1 million.

PRE-TAX RETURN FOR BROWN BAGGING

In order to invest $2,000, you have to earn close to $3,000 before taxes, assuming a roughly 33 percent total tax bite. Suppose, instead of investing those already-taxed dollars, you put that $3,000 into your tax-deferred 401(k)?

- At 6 percent, after 20 years, you'd have about $115,000; after thirty years, nearly $250,000; and after forty years, close to half-a-million.

- At 10 percent, the effect is multiplied: after twenty years you'd have saved about $185,000; after thirty years, about $535,000; and after forty years, about $1.5 million.

If you want to calculate how much you lose in opportunity cost to indulge in your favorite convenience or other habitual but unnecessary expense (cigarettes, candy, lottery tickets, and so on), go to Google and type in "compound interest calculator" and you will find several very simple forms online where you can plug in your annual cost, the return you might expect, and the number of years. I assure you that whatever it is, you'll be shocked.

If you want to persuade someone how much it costs to smoke cigarettes, show them that a pack-a-day habit over twenty years could be costing them more than $100,000 in pre-tax earnings. Such is the power of compounding.

Every financial choice you make has a hidden ripple effect on your financial future. A dollar of lost opportunity today is worth many dollars of added wealth down the road.

BEGIN WITH SIMPLE CHOICES

The road to financial independence begins with the smallest possible step. Decide what you can change, make a plan, and begin to save automatically. If your goal is retirement, look at your employer's 401(k) plan first. If you want to build wealth to finance your life, look at insurance.

Every financial choice you make has a hidden ripple effect on your financial future. A dollar of lost opportunity today is worth many dollars of added wealth down the road.

THE SINGLE DECISION SOLUTION

When you buy a first home, you commit to write 360 checks toward your savings account with a single decision. When you sign up for a retirement account, you commit to writing 840 checks toward savings over a thirty-five year working career. This simple single decision is perhaps the easiest and most important step toward financial independence.

In my own financial life, I have accumulated five properties utilizing the concepts explained in this book. Every time I purchased a new property, it came with its share of stress and anxiety over how I was going to make payments. I reassured my wife that by strapping myself with another mortgage payment,

I reassured my wife that by strapping myself with another mortgage payment, we were accumulating wealth. Every month, before we spent any money on luxuries, we made our mortgage payments. Every property was a forced decision to save.

we were accumulating wealth. Every month, before we spent any money on luxuries, we made our mortgage payments. Every property was a forced decision to save.

About six years ago, I devised the insurance strategy I have explained here. I refinanced all of my properties with interest-only mortgages and bought a life insurance policy equal to the principal I was paying. Then, for the first time in my life, I drove the same car for ten years rather than trade it in on a new model after five.

The first year, I had enough money to pay my annual premium on my life insurance plan and committed to saving the difference between my old mortgage payments and my new, lower mortgage payments. A year later, when my annual bill came from my insurance contract, I found that I had not followed through on the savings part of the plan.

Panicked and depressed that my strategy failed due to my lack of discipline, I searched for a simpler solution. I realized that I didn't need to come up with twelve months of payments but only one month, if I made the decision to put it on automatic debit from my checking. I set up monthly payments from my bank account. That simple decision was made more than six years ago and to this day I have never thought about it or missed the money. Instead, I managed to live on less.

Learning to live on less, and save more, also helps when you reach retirement. You will discover that you have more for retirement, and need less to live on in retirement.

The best way to guarantee discipline is to make one decision and make it automatic.

21 The Foolish Old Man Who Moved Mountains

> **A diamond is a piece of coal that stuck to the job.**
> —Michael Larsen, literary agent

PERSISTENCE, DETERMINATION, AND STEADINESS are hallmarks of all lasting human endeavors, and wealth creation is no exception. The Chinese can trace their civilization back through 5,000 years of continuous history and their ancient philosophers left them a number of wise sayings and fables that express this idea well. One of the most-quoted is the tale of the foolish old man who moved mountains. The message is along the lines of the moral of the race between the rabbit and the hare, but perhaps a bit more colorful.

The story goes that an old farmer had grown tired of having to carry his produce around two large mountains that stood between his fields and the local village where he sold his goods. He decided one day that he and his sons would move the mountains out of the way, to shorten their trek to market.

One day, while the men were shoveling dirt into baskets and hauling it off, the local landlord came by and, when told what the old farmer and his sons were up to, scoffed. "You are a foolish old man," the landlord said. "You will never be able to move those mountains. They are too big and you are but one man."

The old farmer, barely pausing as his heaved another shovelful of earth, replied, "Yes, you are correct. I will never see these mountains moved. But I will work until I die, and my sons will work until they die, and their sons, and their grandsons, and all our descendants will work at it until, one day, we will have moved the mountains."

The Chinese have a similar attitude about money. They are relentless savers, squirreling away an average of 50 percent of their earnings.

We Americans could learn a lot from this aspect of Chinese culture. Instead of seeing the big picture and planning for the distant and inevitable future, we want results now, and we want those results to be spectacular. We suffer from a lottery mentality. We want the new "new" thing, the chance to leapfrog the pack.

The message I try to convey to clients, which I have tried to illustrate in "The Ten Truths of Wealth Creation," is that wise choices plus discipline is the shortest route to your financial independence. In this sense, I hope to undo some of the damage that is done by investment books that advocate strategies for getting rich quickly or by concentrating on a particular investment vehicle, such as real estate. I especially hope to expose the false promises made by an investment industry that is rife with conflicts-of-interest while peddling investment "products" that enrich others at your expense.

For successful wealth creation, the "why" is more important than the "how."

THE FOUR "C"S OF WEALTH CREATION

After all is said and done, there are four basic messages imbedded in all I've tried to explain:

Clarity: My mission as a financial guide is to provide clarity in the decision process. If you can't understand the rationale behind the decisions you're being urged to make about your money, something's wrong.

Complexity: It's my goal to reduce the confusion that comes with investing in today's marketplace. When you find yourself overwhelmed by the details of your financial life, you cannot make smart choices and you become susceptible to misleading marketing pitches.

Certainty: There is no reason that an individual investor shouldn't enjoy the same advantages of corporations and financial institutions that insist on a high degree of predictability in their returns. My hope is to show you how you can reach the outcome you desire without feeling compelled to take extra risks.

Confidence: Just as I showed my father and thousands of others how to unlock hidden wealth, retire early, or reach any other financial goal, there is no reason why you shouldn't enjoy a high level of confidence that your financial plan is going to work. Once you have that confidence, you can concentrate on enjoying your life and reaching your personal potential.

TEN TRUTHS OF WEALTH CREATION

If you can remember most of the Ten Truths as you make your financial decisions in life, you'll begin to see how all your choices can be better informed, independent of misleading advice, and how you can create a future that is secure with reduced anxiety.

1. The key to wealth is through ownership and control, not financial products.
2. The more money moves, the more wealth is created.
3. Everything in life has a cost and requires payments.
4. The biggest cost to wealth—up to 60 percent—is lost opportunity cost: uncaptured interest income, unnecessary interest expense, and failure to manage taxes.
5. Rates of return and index investing as financial planning tools are misleading and meaningless.
6. Insurance is a contract, and understanding this concept is the key to creating and preserving wealth.
7. Risk is not about losing money, but about losing opportunity for profit.
8. Some debt is good, if you finance a thing no longer than its useful life.
9. The biggest obstacle to building wealth is the absence of reliable market information.
10. Financial independence begins with understanding and focusing on your life goals, as opposed to financial goals, and minimizing your future decisions.